ALSO BY
CHARLEY WOOD

A Chateau in Provence

A Villa in Tuscany

A Cottage in the Cotswolds

A Cottage in the Cotswolds

Charley Wood

European Experiences Publishing

Copyright 2013

A Cottage in the Cotswolds

First published in 2013 in the USA by European Experiences Publishing.

Copyright by Charley Wood, 2013

All rights reserved. No part of this publication may be reproduced except by permission of the copyright holder.

The right of Charley Wood to be identified as the author of this work has been asserted by him in accordance with the Copyright, Design, and Patents Act of 1988.

All characters in this book are fictional and any resemblances to real persons living or dead are coincidental.

ISBN-10: 1492913243
EAN-13: 9781492913245

www.european-experiences.com

www.luberonexperience.com

A Cottage in the Cotswolds

www.charleywoodbooks.com

My sincere gratitude to those who patiently read the manuscript of this book and provided valuable suggestions for its improvement – Diane Nevill, Jeanne Draughn, Chris Coburn, Carol Carson, Roz Ault, and Dale Davis.

Cover picture by Eleanor Cox

www.eleanorcox.com

A Cottage in the Cotswolds

Chapter One

New York City

Eddie Fairfax hunched over his quirky, second-hand computer and squinted at the cryptic figures on the screen, his fingers flying over the worn keys with a skill sharpened in years of practice. He sat by the only window in his tired, third floor walk-up. The humble view it gave was of a neglected neighborhood on Manhattan's far north fringe and the thin light that filtered in was accompanied by the blare and clatter of endless street noise. The room's only other light, a bare bulb at the end of a frayed cord, hung just above his head.

The occasional waft of air through the half-opened window made the bulb swing erratically, the dancing shadows giving him the curiously ironic look of a Neanderthal bent over his flickering fire at some primitive task. He'd grown accustomed to the shadows bouncing along the wall and the way they seemed to mimic the movement of his hands over the keyboard.

Then suddenly, the shadows and his hands fell quiet and motionless together. A thin smile played across his lips. He had just finished writing the last lines of software code that would change his life, that would make it better than it had been for the past four years.

But then the past four years, he ruefully conceded, made a pretty low bar to measure his future hopes by. He took a deep breath and pushed his chair back from the makeshift desk, something he'd thrown together using an old door and a couple of large cardboard boxes. He was tired, his shoulders ached, but he was eager and impatient to try out his new creation, to give it the ultimate test.

And he had decided from the very beginning exactly what that test was going to be.

Eddie leaned back in the cheap plastic lawn chair that completed his office ensemble, stretched his arms above his head and absently took stock of the dingy apartment he'd barely had enough cash to rent a few weeks before. Now, he was feeling better - even confident - about his prospects of making this depressing couple of rooms a short-term address.

The few pieces of threadbare furniture that came with the place were not exactly the spark to his optimism. Eddie's relatively good cheer was driven by other considerations. He was confident that he had produced a very clever product and he wanted to share his good news.

He turned in his chair and noticed that the apartment's other resident had quietly returned with cat-like stealth while he was concentrating on his work and was now stretched out on the old sleeper-sofa, snoring softly. He would have to wait a while to share his good news.

He smiled at the absurd but comical scene a few feet behind him. One leg and one arm were flung across the back of the sofa and the other two limbs dangled over the seat. With her head back and mouth slightly agape, the whole image reminded him of a big lanky cat begging to have its stomach rubbed.

The wild, henna-colored hair and hot pink toenails belonged to Vickie. The green and yellow tattoo that crawled down the skin of her throat and disappeared under a tie-dyed t-shirt soon reappeared on the arm that hung over the bottom edge of the seat. Eddie wasn't crazy about tattoos. When he had asked her why she had a tattoo of a salamander on her chest, she replied that since she had no recollection of getting it, she couldn't be expected to know why she had it. That was the kind of thought process that seemed so sensible to Vickie but one that Eddie was still trying to understand since the day they had met.

Eddie sometimes thought that Vickie was a good addition to his life, but just as often, he would have his doubts. She could be moody, stubborn, and undependable. And she had definitely showed herself to be unpredictable, a trait that had already cost Eddie a black eye courtesy of a neighbor who had felt insulted by Vickie's comments. But she could also be considerate and even funny. She was definitely an enthusiastic and creative lover and that made up for a lot of other faults in Eddie's opinion.

He was still trying to learn which Vickie was going to wake up on any given morning. Whenever he'd guessed the wrong answer to that question, she might respond with icy silence or a fiery tongue. Eddie made a point of trying hard to anticipate the right answer.

He knew nothing of any family she might have; she never talked about personal things. He didn't even know her last name. He'd asked her that question on the day they first met. Her answer was, "It's just Vickie." He had thought several times of asking the question again but decided that it really didn't matter. Her aversion to giving up too much information about herself worked the other way, too. That he liked about her. She didn't ask him about his family, work, or his previous life and seemed happy enough to have a place to live and someone for sex.

After four years of not even seeing a woman at Prestonburg, that was okay with Eddie. Vickie had shown only one instance of curiosity. She told him she just loved his accent and asked where he was from. When he told her that he was English, she gave him a broad smile and said that she loved everything about England. She offered no explanation of that statement and Eddie didn't ask.

He wondered if she would still like him - still love everything English - if she ever learned his secret. And he knew that was a revelation he would never, ever make to her.

Vickie, along with the threadbare furniture, had come with the apartment. When Eddie had responded to an ad, 'apartment for rent, cash only, apply in person,' he had found her standing in the corridor outside her door in a yelling match with her landlord. Her arms were wind-milling in sync with her shouts and the landlord, a short disheveled man, had worked himself into an equally agitated state. He was loudly insisting that she had to leave immediately for non-payment of rent. She was yelling just as loudly that she had no money to pay the rent and no place to go.

The situation appeared to be pretty much a draw until Eddie flashed a small wad of cash. The landlord made an easy and quick decision. The sight of so much cash reminded him that it was time to play his trump card. He pulled an envelope from his pocket and waved it in Vickie's face. It was an eviction notice, he told her; she had no choice but to go. The police would be there to enforce the legal document. Eddie noticed that Vickie never had a chance to examine the document since the landlord gave it another quick flourish in front of her face and stuffed it back in his pocket. But it was enough; defeat showed in her eyes and she retreated back into the apartment, apparently to pack. Eddie and the landlord followed.

After a twenty-second tour and a short rundown of the rules, Eddie gave the man most of the cash he'd saved over the past four years. It barely covered the deposit and two month's rent. The landlord, apparently late for other, more urgent matters, was leaving it up to Eddie to finish the eviction.

Vickie waited until the landlord was out of sight, put on her best smile and asked if she could stay. A momentary sense of guilt prompted Eddie to say yes. Now, he looked at her splayed out on the couch and remembered their short history with mixed feelings.

His thirtieth birthday had just passed. There had been no celebration. There had been no reason for one. He had simply observed the day as a boundary line that separated one unmemorable year from the next. He hadn't even bothered to tell Vickie it was his birthday. Why make a fuss about it, he thought. Having her wish him a happy birthday wouldn't do him any good, wouldn't solve his problem. That was one of the things he liked about Vickie – it didn't seem necessary to share his feelings with her, especially the very private ones.

It was especially good not having to talk about his problem. Talking about it would mean thinking about it, and it seemed the more he thought about his problem, the less clear it all became. Just thinking about it was utterly distracting - even painful. And thinking about a solution had been nothing but an exercise in frustration and discouragement. And he had dwindling confidence that he'd recognize a solution even if he saw one.

What he was certain of, however, was that he could trace the beginning of his problem to a single cause and he had the meager comfort of knowing that none of it was his fault. He realized that other people occasionally had problems, too, but most of them were able - it seemed quite unfairly - to root out the cause, change a few things, and get on with a new and better life.

Eddie hadn't been able to duplicate that success.

The genesis of Eddie's problem went way back – exactly thirty years. He knew with unwavering conviction what had caused all the misfortunes in his life, and he knew with equal certainty who was responsible. Every ounce of blame pointed straight to his father. Just thinking about it usually brought the taste of gall to his mouth; to actually hear it said out loud, felt unpleasantly like real, physical pain. This offensive thing in his life was a series of words, six to be exact.

His name.

Eddie Fairfax was, in fact, Edward Algernon Heathcliff Montague Finbar Fairfax.

Eddie hated the name with a vehemence that matched his feeling for the schoolyard bullies and a hundred other tormenters who had used his name like a club to verbally mistreat, abuse, and laugh at him. Eddie was amazed at how a name could elicit such ridicule and sometimes wondered if a real beating with real clubs wouldn't have been a lesser thing to bear. That kind of wound eventually healed, the scars grew faint and the experience dimmed with time. But his was not a problem so easily fixed and the burden of living with his name had made his youth an unhappy and miserable experience. He had always gone to great lengths to hide the unnecessary parts of his name but they seemed to burst forth at the most inopportune times.

As well as his poor mother could figure out - she had once told him - his father had given him the name out of spite towards her while she was recovering from Eddie's birth. His father had then promptly left town never to be heard from again.

The combination of living with such an awkward and embarrassing name and without the guidance of a real father set Eddie upon a course that would eventually put him at odds with the law in several countries, most particularly in England, the land of his birth. Schoolyard brawls became a routine part of his life. Even as Eddie's pugilistic skills advanced, there was always someone new to taunt him.

The funny looks and snickers of his female classmates convinced him that any effort to win a girlfriend would end badly for him. He could handle the physical pain of slugging it out with the boys in his class but he worried that the kind of pain a girl could inflict would be much worse, something like that he'd seen so often in his mother's eyes when he was a child.

The most unforgettable memory he held of his mother was not of her voice, or her face, or even her touch. It was the unsettling sense that he could look into her eyes and peer through and even behind them, to somewhere deeper where the hurt overfilled some reservoir in her, ready to burst forth and overwhelm him. The memory simply brought him back each time to the beginning - his problem.

Occasionally, Eddie had even entertained the idea of changing his name, but that took money – money he didn't have. And since most of the time, his name was his only possession, being totally possession-less was equally hard to contemplate. His name was like an abusive parent or spouse – impossible to live with, unthinkable to live without.

Now after thirty years, Eddie felt he was about to gain some control over his own destiny. The software program he'd worked for months to perfect promised both the money to have more than bare basics and the chance to find some answers to the problem that had wearied him for so long. Most of all, it promised another kind of boundary – one that separated the last four years from the future; his past from the rest of his life.

He thought back to another birthday, his twenty-sixth. Fate had dealt Eddie another low blow that year. Irony had added insult to insult when he acquired a new addition to his name that magnified the burden already hanging about his shoulders like an unbearable, suffocating weight. Sometimes when he looked in a mirror, he'd steal a second glance, worried that something that felt so real might actually be visible and offensive to others, another something to cause him more worry and anguish.

On the very day of his twenty-sixth birthday, it became necessary for Eddie to append the number 182899367 to his other names. The un-exceptional, nine-digit number was his new identification at Prestonburg State Correctional Facility in up-state New York.

A recent emigrant to the United States, Eddie had hoped for a new start. Although prudence had dictated that he should both leave England and find a different way of making a living, Eddie did the one but failed to find a different occupation in his new country.

Unfortunately, he had no other training, no other skills that he felt an employer was likely to pay for, so he continued in the one occupation he knew. He had come to hope that America really was the amazing land of opportunity that he'd heard so much about and that by simply taking a more cautious approach, he could succeed in America and steer clear of the problems he had gotten caught up with in London's tough, east-end neighborhood, the ugly side of Her Majesty's capital that had been his lifelong home.

But that wasn't to be.

In the course of pursuing his everyday business, Eddie had unexpectedly come across another person with the name of Edward M. Fairfax. This unfortunate encounter had at first aroused a feeling of sympathy in Eddie. It was like secretly living with an embarrassing congenital disease for your entire life and then one day discovering there was another human being who had the same indelicate condition. It was both a relief and a disappointment – relief in finding that you were not alone in your suffering and a disappointment that you were no longer special. Eddie had felt that it made him different – a victim patiently enduring another's unearned malice - and occasionally even saw his condition as a comfort.

Eddie was sorry for someone who - he felt sure - had most likely suffered as he had, who had felt the brunt of the same dumb jokes and had endured the same ridicule all because of a name. But his sympathy turned out to be short-lived when it dawned on him that the other Edward M. Fairfax didn't seem to be saddled with all the extra, burdensome names. Eddie's sympathy was further blunted by the need for some quick cash, and his new 'acquaintance' could help out in that respect. Why should he treat Edward, he reasoned, any differently than he treated others.

Sympathy had to be put aside, for business was business, and Eddie's business was stealing other people's identity and eventually their money.

Identity theft was the term used by the police, but Eddie chose a more expansive way of looking at it; the public was merely a horde of faceless strangers being cheated and bamboozled at every turn by merchants, governments, and even friends and family. So why shouldn't he have his turn? He saw no harm in sharing in the good fortune of others. It was also a kind of justice he told himself. Laugh at me if you want, but I'll have the last laugh.

The police called his method skimming, but Eddie looked upon it as just another use of modern technology.

Eddie had at one time been hampered by a small kernel of conscience and had tried to justify to himself his chosen way of making a living. His victims were mere strangers he reasoned, and yeah, it would hurt a bit when he tapped their bank accounts, but they'd get over it. What he was doing, he told himself, was no different from what millions of other people did when they sold worthless products or charged for work they didn't do. He simply had a different approach. But eventually, he gave up this kind of unprofitable thinking and quit worrying about people he'd never meet. He had to make a living while he concentrated on solving his problem.

The primary tools of Eddie's trade were two small devices. One fit into an ATM's card slot and the other fit over the ATM's keypad. The two devices enabled him to record account numbers and passwords of unsuspecting bank customers as they blithely went about extracting their money from the machines.

Eddie used this information to fabricate duplicate ATM cards and then moved about the greater New York metropolitan area withdrawing money from his mark's account until either the victim or the bank realized what was going on and froze the account, or changed passwords. Eddie would then destroy the cards and go on to the next person on his list.

In a city the size of New York, with its teeming streets and thousands of ATMs, it was next to impossible to catch someone like Eddie and the banks grudgingly bore the costs and accepted skimming as an unfortunate but inevitable cost of doing business.

But it was another quirky part of Eddie's personality that wouldn't let him completely put the other Edward M. Fairfax out of his thoughts. Eddie had a curiosity that, once sparked, could smolder like a banked fire until it burst into flame at the most unexpected moment. The very idea of another Edward M. Fairfax out there in the world haunted him, infused his dreams.

He imagined that Edward had faced the same irksome problems in life that he had but was jealous when he also imagined that Edward had worked through them. Did Edward worry to distraction as he did, or had he somehow found a means to cope? Perhaps fate had simply been harsher on himself than on Edward. Eddie's feelings about Edward alternated between contempt and pity, between bitterness and compassion.

Eddie couldn't accept the idea of coincidence; he didn't believe in it. If there were obvious causes for the ordinary events in life, Eddie was even more convinced that extraordinary events were propelled by extraordinary causes, never by chance. That he had unexpectedly found another Edward M. Fairfax was indeed extraordinary. What were the odds, he wondered, of two different fathers - out of spite - naming their sons Edward Algernon Heathcliff Montague Finbar Fairfax?

Eddie hadn't been able to determine with certainty that the *M* in Edward's name actually stood for Montague, or even that Edward had all the other names, but Eddie had obsessed and agonized for so long over his name and its wearisome problems that he was almost certain that the *M* could stand for nothing else.

Grudgingly, Eddie had to acknowledge that Edward had somehow been able to shed the other, excess baggage from his name. That brought new feelings of envy and resentment.

Or maybe, he thought as he continued to turn this over in his head, the other father had had the decency to leave out the most offensive names. Or had he? Eddie sometimes wondered if the two fathers were, in fact, the same sick individual leaving his pathetic sort of humor moldering in his wake, slightly altering the name for whatever perverted reason made sense only to him.

Eddie constantly thought about what he'd do if he ever met his father. He was sure beyond doubt that he would recognize him. And then, what? Would he confront him and demand an apology, some form of reparation or measure of justice? Eddie had imagined a thousand different scenerios. None seemed to promise relief.

Eddie's mother had reluctantly conceded that his father had been a dashingly handsome man who could turn a woman's head even as he was walking out the door. At least, Eddie thought, he could be thankful for that. His old man had bequeathed him uncommonly good looks, a tall muscular frame, thick dark hair, a strong chin and well set eyes.

As hard as he tried not to, his thoughts kept straying back to the other Edward Fairfax, and Eddie wondered what he might be like. Would he instinctively recognize him if he saw Edward on the street? Would there be a resemblance and what would that mean?

Eddie soon stumbled onto another business opportunity that offered a way to satisfy his curiosity about Edward. Once he secured the needed information from his ATM scanner, Eddie was a virtual *artiste* when it came to making the cards he needed to drain other people's bank accounts. His cards were practically indistinguishable from the real thing and almost always worked. In an attempt to grow his little enterprise, he occasionally provided the valuable service of fabricating these cards for other acquaintances to the same end.

One day, over a few beers in a back corner of Eddie's favorite bar, an acquaintance offered to teach him how to hack into other people's email accounts. His drinking partner laughingly referred to this activity as something he did for 'a lot of fun but very little profit.' All Eddie had to do was to make a couple dozen plastic cards to go with the account numbers and PINs the acquaintance would supply.

Eddie immediately saw a different value in such knowledge. He could find out everything he wanted to know about Edward. What would someone with a name like that do for a living? Maybe he did what Eddie did. No, Eddie had already decided. The other Edward didn't have a lot of money but it came in regular, monthly deposits. The guy had a real job. He might have a normal and decent life, a girlfriend, a car, even a house.

Although Eddie was lately beginning to admire and even like Edward, he couldn't totally fight off a lingering resentment. Somehow Edward had adapted and overcome their common problem, a problem that had been a source of such torment for Eddie. Edward had somehow succeeded where Eddie hadn't been able to. In spite of the growing affinity he felt for Edward - even verging on something like friendship - Eddie still managed to make a big dent in Edward's bank account before Edward and his bank finally caught on.

Normally, at this point, Eddie would have shredded or burned the card and moved on – practically immune to any consequences. But the thought of knowing more about the other Edward Fairfax was a temptation he couldn't resist. He didn't understand why he felt so curious about Edward or why Edward had become so important to him. He kept asking himself why he cared, why it mattered. But then, suddenly, he realized why.

It was so obvious, a moment of crystal clarity - Edward could provide him the answer.

The answer to how he had overcome, how he had adapted, how he had managed to get along in life despite his problem, and then he, Eddie, could replicate the solution and find his long sought relief.

Although Eddie was determined to find a solution, he was becoming less and less clear about the question he was trying so hard to answer. Were his problems the result of his long, cumbersome and ridiculous name? He'd been so certain for so long but now some doubts were creeping in. It was, after all, just a name. And had it been the same for Edward? Had he constantly been at odds with schoolmates, had he been laughed at by fellow workers, had the opposite sex ridiculed and avoided him? Or was the real question something else that he hadn't yet thought about? Perhaps Edward would be able to help with that, too.

With a hundred other areas in his life where he needed help, it was in this most important area where Eddie had been totally unable to formulate a question that made enough sense to even suggest where to look for a solution. Any time he thought so long and hard about it, he usually got a pounding headache and wished fervently that his name was John Doe.

The one thing he was absolutely certain about, any answer would have to make a difference in his life or it was not an answer. Now, he thought, he at least had a starting point. It was all so very complicated, Eddie worried, but he was sure that it was soon to become much clearer and Edward was the key.

Eddie's innate belief in a cause and effect order to everything in life assured him that the one would some-how follow the other. His name had been the cause of all his problems and, unfortunately, he knew all the effects. Edward would certainly understand the problem and Eddie was encouraged by the knowledge that Edward had found the answer. If Edward could be per-suaded to share with Eddie how he had overcome his own problems, then Eddie could have the hope of doing the same.

Eddie set about learning more about Edward - where he lived, what he did for a living, but most of all what he was like as a person; how he had held up under the strain of living with that name - their name. He needed to talk to Edward. He was becoming more and more convinced that only Edward could help, only Edward would understand.

Eddie's curiosity finally burned too hot. In trying to get closer to Edward, he got careless. When he tried to approach Edward directly, he threw away all caution and he got caught. A police search of his apartment found stacks of blank plastic cards that Eddie couldn't explain, of account numbers he shouldn't have, and much more cash than Eddie could possibly have earned. Eddie was bundled off to a New York City jail and for the next three-and-a-half months wondered if Edward knew what had happened to him and waited to talk to his attorney.

At his trial, Eddie had hoped for - even half way expected - understanding and sympathy from Edward. After all, they shared something in common, something immensely important. They were a brotherhood of two. Of all Eddie's marks, Edward would the only one there to testify at his trial. That was the only encouraging bit of information he had gleaned from one very brief meeting with his court-appointed attorney.

Eddie expected Edward to be his lone advocate and was touched by this uncommon support and took great comfort from that knowledge. How could it be otherwise? Apparently, Edward had known all along what had happened. He'd be there when he was needed.

On the day of his trial, Eddie looked over the few people in the courtroom and tried to decide which one was Edward. To have a friend there to see him through a tough time was something Eddie had never experienced before. And he had immediately recognized Edward the moment he walked into the courtroom. The resemblance was unmistakable which was really no surprise to Eddie. He'd often imagined how their first meeting would play out, perhaps like a reunion of long-separated brothers. An instant eye contact, a brief smile of undeniable recognition, a bond unspoken but certain and firm.

Lawyers stood and read complicated and lengthy texts and passed and shuffled stacks of documents and Eddie found himself excitedly anticipating hearing Edward on the witness stand. He'd have a pleasant, yet strong and commanding voice, Eddie was certain. His would be a voice the jurors would listen to, a voice they'd believe.

At length, Eddie heard the bailiff call Edward Fairfax to the stand. Eddie watched Edward just in case he should offer a smile in his direction as he rose from his seat, a sure sign of his support. Edward neither moved nor smiled in Eddie's direction when his name was called. Eddie waited. Edward hadn't heard his name called, Eddie thought. He looked back toward the bailiff, sure he'd call out Edward's name again.

Instead, Eddie noticed a thin balding man hesitantly rise from a seat several rows back. The man scurried toward the witness stand like a small animal running for the cover of its burrow and he seemed to be looking away from Eddie. Eddie was momentarily confused. Why had this man come forward when Edward had been called? Eddie soon realized his mistake, something was terribly wrong. The man sat on the edge of the chair, raised his hand and swore that his name was Edward M. Fairfax. He also swore to tell the truth.

If his hopes and expectations had had any different outcome - Eddie would later admit – he would have been surprised. His usual luck had held up. He'd hoped for a friend, but what he got instead was an angry and vindictive witness against him. The thin man accused and railed at him and pointed in his direction. He threw sharp stares and harsh words but they could as well have been sharp stones and arrows. Eddie was not only shocked, he felt betrayed. This was not the Edward he had imagined, the Edward from whom he had hoped to see sympathy and understanding.

Eddie had thought that by telling part of his own story on the stand, the jury would understand what he had struggled with and extend him appropriate mercy. But after being intimidated and verbally beat up by an incensed, fast talking prosecutor, Eddie was dazed and looked about the courtroom for help from any quarter. His own lawyer was already packing up his briefcase, glancing at his watch. He was further dismayed that the *real* Edward he had so easily recognized was no longer there. Why had he left, Eddie worried, had the proceedings been too much for him too?

By the time the bailiff had escorted Eddie to the men's room and back, the jury had already returned to their seats. The jury foreman stood, gave Eddie a scathing look and cruelly quashed any faint hopes he still clung to. The words "guilty, guilty, guilty" reverberated inside Eddie's head like a gong and when the steel cuffs closed around his wrists, he finally realized that his trust in Edward had been sorely misplaced.

The judge squinted at Eddie, ground his teeth and gave him the maximum sentence. Eddie could see it in the judge's eyes, the withering look of revenge, the same contempt he saw glaring at him from the jury box. Eddie could only conclude that the judge had lost money to someone like himself and recognized an easy chance for revenge. The terrible realization hit him like an electric current, he was going to take the rap for the judge's loss, too.

It was a nightmare that wouldn't go away. The memory of that moment had endlessly tormented Eddie as the days turned into weeks and the weeks into months at Prestonburg, a medium security prison perched on a bleak and rocky peninsula jutting out from New York's eastern shore of Lake Ontario. The summers were short, the winters long and brutal, and the facility itself a hundred years out of date; all the ingredients for a miserable four years.

But that time and place was now behind him. He stretched his tired arms one more time, glanced back at the still sleeping Vickie and returned his attention to the computer screen. He felt the sense of satisfaction all over again and decided that his time at Prestonburg hadn't been all bad.

He'd had plenty of opportunity to hone his skills, to learn where he had made mistakes and where he could be more careful and productive. Eddie's British dialect had caught the attention of the warden who was of the opinion that someone with a foreign sounding accent might add a little class to the drab environment of a prison office in rural New York State. Eddie's talents wouldn't be wasted in the laundry or the kitchen or in painting something that had already been painted a hundred times. He was assigned to clerical duties and was allowed to make himself useful in a small office right next to the warden's.

Eddie had access to a computer, something which was specifically forbidden by the judge's sentencing decree. When he was processed in, that part was either never read or conveniently ignored, and Eddie recognized an opportunity to work on his 'degree' that he'd need when he 'graduated' in four years.

There had been a terrible moment early on in his 'studies.' He'd finished a small project the warden had him working on and was using his computer time to refine his hacking skills. Eddie had been so absorbed in what he was doing that he hadn't noticed the presence behind him. He almost fainted when a steel-hard hand clamped down on his shoulder from behind and a voice hissed in his ear, "Whadda ya working on, Heathcliff Montague Finbar?"

The hand swung him sharply around and a heavy boot planted itself with a resounding thud on the chair squarely between Eddie's legs. The captain of the prison guards bent down until his florid face hung inches away from Eddie's nose, "So, you're looking to stay here for a couple of extra years, is that right?"

The stale, tobacco breath was repulsive enough, but the threat of having to spend an extra day in the place made his stomach knot up and practically do a flip. And then a worse blow. "I could tell everyone just who we have here at good old Prestonburg, couldn't I, Mr. Edward Algernon Heathcliff Montague Finbar Fairfax. Eddie's persecutor spit out the names like they were some obnoxious taste he couldn't get out of his mouth, and with the disgusting mouth so close to Eddie's face, it seemed his name now reeked of a foul stench. The guard's wheezing laugh was just another blade twisting in his gut.

Eddie's face drained of all color and he was unable to make any response. The guard took down his boot that had come so close to damaging Eddie's manhood and looked behind himself as if to make sure whatever he was planning for Eddie had no witnesses. Eddie already knew that the warden had left for the day and was afraid that the guard was just waiting to have some perverse fun at his expense. Satisfied that they were alone, the guard stared hard at Eddie and Eddie waited for the hammer to fall. The guard jerked another chair to where it directly faced Eddie and dropped his considerable bulk onto it.

"I'm gonna do you a great big favor, see, and keep this little secret of yours a secret. And you're gonna do me a little favor, too, you understand?"

The guard gave Eddie a sharp punch in the chest for emphasis. His fist was huge and the blow had a hammer behind it. It took Eddie's breath away, but he managed to nod his head up and down enough to communicate his agreement. A couple of more years spent here with every other con laughing at his name was worse than death. They might as well shoot him now. Whatever the guard wanted, Eddie wanted it, too. Even more. He nodded his head a little more vigorously. Eddie remembered that at that moment, his heart was beating like it was going to burst through his chest.

Now he could look back on that moment as one of the rare lucky breaks in his life.

Apparently the guard had secretly observed Eddie at his 'studies' for several days and had made the effort to check up on him; to see what had landed him at Prestonburg. The guard offered to keep Eddie's secret in return for Eddie's help in a little scam the guard was running of his own.

From that day, Eddie had all the computer time he wanted as well as internet access. The petty gambling operation the guard was running was peanuts as far as Eddie was concerned, but it was a turning point for him. He now had a protector and all the time he needed to plan his revenge.

His thoughts were pulled back to the present by a little grunt from behind him. He gave another quick glance in the direction of the couch. He very much wanted to tell Vickie his good news, but would wait until she woke on her own; she was grumpy when she didn't get her sleep.

He rubbed his tired eyes and turned back to the flickering screen. As he contemplated what appeared to be nothing more than a confusion of obscure letters, numbers, and symbols, he felt a perverse pride. The lines of computer language that glowed on the screen were every bit as much a masterpiece as any museum-hung canvas filled with skillful brushstrokes in paint.

He thought about what had brought him to this point - a lot of dumb mistakes, a lot of bad luck, and a big bill to pay. Yeah, he'd paid for what he'd done and probably paid for whatever the judge figured somebody owed him, too.

Eddie could still remember the look in the judge's eyes right after the foreman of the jury said, "We find the defendant guilty as charged." The anger and seething hate were unmistakable, and Eddie could almost feel the judge putting a noose around his neck with his pale, scrawny hands. Eddie was halfway expecting a few extra months just because of his name. Luckily, that didn't happen and Eddie quietly did his time with the exception of the one little incident.

And now it was time to get even, especially with the judge. It was also time to check up on Edward, to see how life was treating him. Hopefully, Eddie thought with a widening grin, Edward had been very successful over the past four years and had managed to save a lot of cash. Eddie had already calculated the amount that each one owed him to make up for lost income and time and four years of misery. Now it was up to the judge and Edward to start making payments on their accounts.

Chapter Two

New York City

E ddie sat staring intently at the computer screen and feeling very good about the results he was getting with his new code. He didn't see the slim hand sneak across his shoulder and give a sharp tug at the tuft of chest hair peeking above his collar. He jumped at the sharp twinge and swatted at the offending hand.

"Jeez, Vickie, why do you do things like that. You scared the crap out of me." He'd just been remembering the steel hand clamped on his shoulder at Prestonburg.

"I thought you liked it," she cooed as she playfully bit on his right earlobe.

He thought of objecting further but he had quickly learned that she would just end up pouting, and Vickie's pouting usually involved slamming doors, throwing things, and in the end, tears. He was too excited by what he was doing to get into an argument with her; he didn't want the distraction. Besides, her nibbling on his ear reminded him that he didn't want to upset her for other reasons.

"I'm hungry," she whispered in his ear. "Sleeping makes me hungry."

"Everything makes you hungry," Eddie shot back. He found it hard to believe that she could eat as much as she did. She ate like someone starved, but never seemed to show it on her lean frame. Anyway, that wasn't important now. He was hungry, too. It felt like hours since they had eaten a less than satisfying breakfast, and it wasn't surprising that she was hungry. Eddie's recent income from his work had barely been enough to cover basic expenses. He had been enslaved to his computer, determined to finish his masterpiece. But now that was done. It was time for a change.

"Put on your best outfit," he told her, "I'm taking you out to a nice restaurant."

"Really," she brightened, "I'll be ready in just a minute." She was already pulling the t-shirt over her head as she turned toward the bedroom.

Eddie couldn't imagine what her best outfit might look like. He'd only seen her in t-shirts and jeans. Come to think of it, that's all he had, too. They would stop at a couple of ATM's on the way to dinner and the both of them could pick up some new clothes. Dinner and new wardrobes would be a gift from the judge.

When he thought of the judge, he had to smile again. There'd definitely be more 'gifts' from the judge. He'd retired since sending Eddie to Prestonburg and was apparently planning to make some kind of major purchase, maybe a little farm or a boat where he could get away from a lifetime of dealing with the dregs of the world.

The judge's checking account had lately been loaded up with thousands of dollars. Funny thing, these dollars hadn't come from any other account under the judge's name as far as Eddie had been able to determine. The routing was convoluted and showed definite signs of offshore origin. Whatever the judge was up to, Eddie didn't really care, but he was going to seriously lighten the judge's account and the fun part was going to be watching the judge's reaction. If Eddie was right, there wouldn't be any reaction. He was betting that a lifetime of being around lawyers and criminals had rubbed off on the judge.

Eddie was now privy to every email the judge sent or received, and he was pretty sure the judge wouldn't and couldn't complain to anybody, even if Eddie took every cent. And that was what he intended to do. Once he had a name and password for one account, his new software program enabled him to find and break into every account that person had in any bank.

"Whadda you think?" came the excited voice from behind him.

Eddie turned around to find Vickie posing like a runway model, one hand perched on her hip and the other leaning against the door frame. A long-sleeve purple t-shirt hid most of the salamander but the color of the baggy green slacks assaulted his eyes like something allowed out of the closet only for St. Patrick's day. The hot pink toenails glowed from the front of her sandals like warning signals. He wasn't sure what to say, but since he had nothing better to change into himself, he let it go with, "Looks great!"

They walked along West 177th street. Eddie loved walking to the point where he could first see the George Washington Bridge, a beautiful structure with a great name. George Washington - now there was a name that Eddie could admire.

He and Vickie stopped at two ATMs along the street and with her as lookout, he set the judge back several hundred dollars, and this was just for starters, he told himself. The judge had run up a pretty big tab and it was going to take a while to settle his account. Eddie remembered one item on the judge's bill in particular.

When Eddie's trial was practically over and he thought he had escaped with only a prison sentence, the judge told him to stand and gave him another look down his long nose, "The defendant, Edward Algernon Heathcliff Montague Finbar Fairfax, is remanded to the custody of the bailiff." The judge spit out every one of Eddie's names as if it were some impossible, unpronounceable language and then slammed his gavel on the bench. When Eddie jumped, the judge gave a snorting laugh. A sickening titter rippled through the courtroom and Eddie's knees felt weak. He almost threw up in a trash can by the defendant's table.

That would cost the judge a considerable premium.

It was still early for dinner in New York so they got in immediately at Ray's Famous Gourmet Diner and took a booth by the front window. In one smooth motion, Vickie grabbed the menu, flipped it open and slid along the bench. Her eyes roved the menu like a predator searching for small animals, muscles taut, anticipating, ready to spring on a helpless steak or thoroughly ravage an entire salad bar. Eddie was amused as he watched her and even more amazed when she ordered. He thought about asking who else was going to join them, but since the judge was paying, he decided to say nothing and even splurge a little bit himself.

Both Eddie and Vickie made up for the past week of skipped and sparse meals and even managed to get in more conversation than they had for the several weeks they had known each other. Neither seemed ready to reveal anything personal, so the conversation revolved around their planned shopping expedition they had put off until the next day. Eating was the primary objective for the time being.

After an epic meal, both leaned back in the comfortable booth and stretched out, satisfied at being full for a change and in no hurry to get back to the apartment. Eddie ordered coffee for both of them.

When the waitress brought their coffee, Eddie interpreted the look on her face as saying she was torn between expecting no tip - probably based on the way they were dressed - and expecting a really big one based on the amount of food they had ordered and consumed. He could understand her concern and confusion. Should she toss their check on the table and go in search of a real tip or should she continue to smile and work this table – she'd already invested a lot of time and effort.

It was a lot to read from a look on someone's face but when the waitress left to get their check, Vickie was apparently thinking the same thing. She leaned across the table toward Eddie.

"Can you leave her a really nice tip, Eddie? She's worked hard."

He smiled at Vickie with a little bit of pride. He'd never heard her express any such sentiment before. "Yeah, sure. He reached in his pocket and brought out the bulge of bills and held it tightly just under the table. It felt comforting just to feel the substantial worth and the purchasing power he held in his hand.

"I used to do this, you know," Vickie said, nodding at the waitress' back as she walked away. "A bunch of different places . . . but it just didn't seem to work out." It sounded like she was finally ready to reveal something about herself but changed her mind in mid-thought. She popped a last bite of bread into her mouth and stared out the window.

"You mean you used to work as a waitress?" Eddie saw the relaxed mood as an opportunity to ask some questions he'd wondered about.

Vickie turned slowly back from looking out the window. Eddie noticed that the salamander's tail was moving. It had been tattooed directly onto the skin over her jugular vein and now her veins stood out and throbbed. Her eyes narrowed and bored into him.

"What?" Eddie asked perplexed. He hadn't seen her look this way before. "It was just a harmless question," he added.

"A harmless question," she growled through clenched teeth. "There are no harmless questions from crazy people, and you're crazy. All you worry about and think about is your stupid name."

He stared at her with his mouth open, shocked at the sharpness of her attack. He hadn't even realized he'd ever talked to her about his problem.

Vickie's tantrum seemed to cool as quickly as it had flared. She gave Eddie a shrug, picked up her coffee and again gazed out the window. He was stung into silence by her verbal assault. He hadn't realized that he had ever said anything about his . . .

While she absently watched the street, he wondered about this tiny glimpse into her life that she had allowed; that she'd had a job or maybe several, but they hadn't worked out. Why hadn't they worked out, he wondered, but not enough to ask further questions. Had that brief view into her life been on purpose or just a little breakdown in her armour? Whatever it was, he'd wait until she decided to say more. That was probably just as well; he'd not have to worry about feeling he needed to answer questions about his own secret.

"Could I take care of this for you?" Eddie heard a voice say behind him. He turned back from the window. The waitress stood there holding out his check. A quick glance told him that they'd ordered just over a hundred, fifty dollars of diner food. That was ok. Their stomachs felt satisfied for the first time in days and the judge was going to be generous. Eddie looked at Vickie as he peeled off bills from the stack he held under the table and laid four fifty-dollar bills on the check. He smiled at the waitress as he said, "Thanks."

Both Vickie and the waitress grinned at each other and decided that Eddie was a generous man. Eddie smiled to himself and thought that's what the judge would have wanted.

Sidewalk traffic was still light as they walked back to the apartment. Stopping at the same ATM's, Eddie used some different cards and pocketed another thousand dollars. Vickie never asked questions about the cards or where they might have come from, but Eddie had noticed her eyeing the growing wad of cash as he added more after each stop. He wasn't anticipating a question but somehow felt like he needed to explain, "We'll need a pretty big chunk of money tomorrow to get us both some decent clothes."

"Yeah, I know." She was excited by the prospect. "But I was wondering if maybe we could start looking for a new apartment."

The word 'we' caught Eddie a little off guard. He hadn't given any thought to there being a 'we.' Vickie had been there from the beginning, but they hadn't talked a lot or spent much time together. Their time at the diner had been the longest they had spent together outside the bedroom and he still knew little more about her than the fact that she had worked as a waitress. He remembered the yelling match between her and her landlord on the day he had gone to answer the ad for the apartment. She confessed to having no money to pay rent but that was it. No excuses and no looking for pity. He liked that about her.

He spent most days working on his computer and she was either sleeping or out somewhere. She didn't tell him where she was going and he didn't ask. Although in

32

the intimate moments after lovemaking he had almost asked several times where she went during the day, but something had kept him from it. Maybe he was afraid to know or maybe it would just open doors to places he didn't want to go.

As they were walking the last block to the apartment, he felt Vickie touch her hand against his and after a moment, take his hand in hers. It felt nice. It had been a long time since he'd held a woman's hand like that.

They walked silently along, dodging other pedestrians. He'd have to think more about the 'we' idea he decided.

"Yeah, that's a good idea," he said. "Let's pick up a paper and start checking the ads."

Back in the apartment, Vickie immediately threw herself on the couch and began noisily turning the pages of the *Times* real estate section. With a full stomach and a pocket full of cash, Eddie went happily back to his computer.

He had made a good start with the judge and now it was time to let Edward start contributing. But it was going to be a special situation with Edward. He should have been more understanding and sympathetic, Eddie thought. Edward had a double debt to pay and Eddie had been doing some special homework. He'd had the time to learn all about Edward. He smiled as he signed into Edward's email account. He probably knew as much about Edward as Edward knew about himself.

Edward wasn't a very active emailer and Eddie hadn't checked his account in a couple of days. There were three new emails since he had last checked. Two were sales come-ons and the third one was from some-one who wasn't one of his regular contacts. The fact that the sender had a .uk email address grabbed Eddie's attention. Edward hadn't opened any of the three, yet, and Eddie had developed a way of opening an email without it showing 'opened' on the owner's account page.

He clicked on the third email and read it. The message was fairly short and to the point. And yet, it left more questions than it answered. He read it again, and finally gave a long, low whistle. Maybe he didn't know as much about Edward as he thought he did. He read it a third time before turning toward Vickie.

"We may need to hold up on getting another apartment," he said as he motioned for her to look at the screen.

"Aw, come on, Eddie, why?" She was already complaining as she dropped the paper on the floor and started toward the computer.

Eddie pointed at the screen. "Looks like my friend has come into a little inheritance."

Vickie walked closer, leaned over his shoulder and read Edward's email. It was the first time that Eddie had let her see what he spent so much time doing on his computer. He waited for her to finish and see what her reaction would be.

"Yeah, so is your middle initial M, too?"

Eddie felt the familiar twinge crawl up his back. "Not that! Didn't you read the email?"

"Yeah, so what?"

"He has an inheritance. It's in England."

Vickie leaned closer and read the message again. "Wow, cool. I love English stuff."

Chapter Three

New York City

E ddie quickly grabbed his pencil and wrote down the name and address of the sender from England. He then sent the email to Edward's spam folder. He wanted time to think through what this could mean before Edward saw it. Maybe Edward didn't need to see it at all.

"Why does this mean we can't get a new apartment," Vickie said a bit sharply as she picked up the Times real estate section from the floor.

"I don't know. Just give me a few minutes to think."

Vickie stood with one hand on her hip and studied Eddie for a moment, trying to decide if he was serious.

She finally threw the paper back on the floor, pouted off to the bedroom and slammed the door behind her.

Eddie wasn't sure how this inheritance business would change his plans for Edward. They not only shared the same name but now it seemed that Edward had some connection to England. Could this mean there was a possible connection between them, or was it just a coincidence. No, Eddie said to himself. He didn't believe in coincidence.

He read it again and deleted the email. He didn't want Edward to see it and didn't forward it to himself because he didn't want an electronic trail pointing in his direction. Eddie had an excellent memory and wrote down verbatim the message from the solicitor in Gloucestershire, England.

It is my duty to be the bearer of both good and bad tidings. As the executor for the estate of the lately deceased Reginald Osbourne Fairfax, I am hereby advising you that a reading of Sir Reginald's last will and testament will be available at your earliest convenience. You, Mr. Fairfax, being Sir Reginald's only known surviving relative and heir should reasonably expect to inherit his entire estate. Please reply forthwith on your travel plans to this office.

Respectfully,
Claiborne Rhetts
Solicitor at Law
crhetts@Dunhamsolicitors.uk
13 New Road, Suite 2278
Moreton-in-Marsh
Gloucestershire GL56 0
England

A hundred questions buzzed in Eddie's head as he read and re-read the message he'd jotted down on the notepad.

Chapter Four

New York City

E ddie could already hear soft snoring sounds coming from behind the closed bedroom door. He picked up the scattered sections of the Times and sat down on the couch. He absently looked at the paper, but the words, *travel plans,* turned over and over in his thoughts and wouldn't let him concentrate on apartments in New York. He tossed the paper back on the floor, closed his eyes and leaned back against the sagging pillows.

If Edward had inherited property in England, Eddie reasoned, then it made perfect sense that Edward was also English, just like him. And they had their name in common, their mutual burden. So much was adding up. What else could there be?

Eddie's eyes flew open and he bolted upright on the couch.

That was it!

It was no coincidence that the email had come at this time. Eddie believed in the timing of things. Timing was important, it always meant something. The inheritance just might be the key to what Eddie was looking for and Edward was going to help him figure that out. More than that, Edward was going to finance his quest.

Eddie was going to England.

He jumped to his feet and was through the bedroom door before he realized the scope of his decision. He sat on the one small part of the bed that wasn't covered by splayed out arms and legs and began to shake Vickie awake.

"Hey, wake up. I'm going to England."

Vickie squinted at him through cat-like eyes and raised up on one elbow, the salamander staring at him, too. "You're what?"

"I'm going to England." He said again, apparently not having thought past that declaration.

"You're taking me, too, right?"

Eddie started to say that that wouldn't be possible when she pulled him down against herself, put her mouth against his ear. She gently bit at his earlobe.

There was no further talk of the trip that night but both Eddie and Vickie knew that a decision had been made. Vickie was going to England, too.

As they stepped onto the sidewalk the next morning, Eddie considered the early May weather to be a positive omen for their plans, a confirmation of a good decision. A gentle sun was just beginning to probe between the buildings, chasing away the last grey of dawn from a cloudless sky. It was warmer in New York at this time of year than anytime Eddie could remember – or maybe it just where in New York he was remembering. An involuntary shiver ran up his back at the memory of winters in Prestonburg. Or maybe, Eddie now worried, it was because of the dark sedan parked at the curb across the street. Two men sat in the front seat. Their attention seemed to be riveted on the entrance of their apartment building.

He hurried Vickie along the sidewalk. They would take the Eighth Avenue line to midtown to do some serious shopping. Now, it wasn't just any old clothes shopping expedition but one specifically for clothes to travel in, he'd told Vickie, hoping she'd settle on a more traditional wardrobe. He desperately hoped there'd be no more purple tees or Kelly green slacks.

They'd stop for a quick breakfast and hit a few ATMs after they got to midtown. Even after an enormous meal last night, they had burned off most of the calories after Eddie had agreed to take Vickie along to England. She'd convinced him of her value as a traveling companion and Eddie had been quick to see her point.

He'd been up early, too excited to sleep, and was at the computer making some changes to Edward's email account when he began to hear rustlings in the bedroom. Vickie was up earlier than usual also.

Eddie changed the settings in Edward's email account so that any message with a .uk origin would go directly to spam. Edward didn't need to know about his good fortune just yet. Eddie also decided to wait on Edward's contribution to his financial needs until later. He didn't want Edward alerted to anything he might need to do.

After taking this precaution to keep Edward in the dark and uninvolved, Eddie could enjoy the day with Vickie and think about the other things he would need to make the trip to England – like a passport.

Eddie and Vickie had a very successful day shopping. He had to admit that Vickie looked quite good in fashionable clothes and since he was still able to tap the judge's account for more cash, he saw no need to be frugal. After the first purchase by both of them, Eddie thought it would be good to get the passport process started. They found the closest Duane Reade drug store and with at least respectable attire up top, had their passport pictures made.

By late afternoon, they had so many bags that Eddie decided they'd never get them all on the metro and took them home by cab. Vickie was thoroughly impressed, she said, it was her first time to ride in a cab.

If she had never been in a cab before, and didn't have a passport, Eddie wasn't surprised when she asked how soon they could leave for England. Could they go tomorrow? She was excited and Eddie was amused by her childlike naivete about travel.

"Not that soon," he laughed. "I've got some things to take care of first."

Eddie noticed the driver looking in the rearview mirror more than someone driving in New York traffic should be doing. He leaned closer to Vickie and whispered, "I think the driver is a little too curious. We'll talk about it when we get back to the apartment." Eddie worried when anyone paid too close attention to him or what he was doing. Prestonburg taught him that usually meant trouble. Eddie had the cab drop them a couple of blocks short of their building just in case the cabbie's interest was more than personal nosiness. He'd also have the chance to look out for the dark sedan and its two curious occupants.

Vickie had started to complain about having to carry the heavy bags for the two blocks, especially when the cab could have brought them right to their door. He was having a hard time concentrating on what he needed to do with Vickie complaining and listened without comment until they were inside the apartment. He had noticed that the dark sedan had vacated its spot and was now replaced by a plumber's van.

"I can't take you to England if you're going to complain about everything. You can just stay here," he told her flatly. "I had him drop us where I did for a reason." Vickie looked hurt but quickly decided that pouting was the better response. She dropped her bags and headed for the bedroom, slamming the door behind her. Eddie had seen this enough in the past few weeks to know she would either be asleep in ten minutes or be back out saying she was sorry. He'd have to wait to see which Vickie responded to this crisis.

He booted up his computer and before the machine had time to demand his password, he heard the bedroom door open. He turned just in time to see Vickie give him one of her glares, reach down and grab the bags and disappear back to the bedroom. That was either a good sign or a bad sign. He didn't really care which at the moment. He needed to check on Edward.

He opened Edward's email account and found no activity from Edward and no further messages from the solicitor in England. Apparently, Eddie thought, the solicitor was satisfied to wait for an answer from Edward. Eddie knew he couldn't wait too long to send back his travel schedule and risk getting another notice from the solicitor. It would be just his luck for that message to slip past the spam blocker and land right in Edward's in-box. He needed to hurry with his preparations. And to do that, Eddie had a little problem to work around.

Surprisingly, his passport had been returned to him when he was released from Prestonburg, but he had this little matter of still being on probation. He had to check in with his probation officer the fifth day of each month, and today was already the twenty-sixth of May. He didn't know what restrictions might be attached to his passport and didn't want to take the chance of finding out at the TSA security check at Kennedy airport. And then there was passport control at Heathrow. The thought of being bundled back on an airplane and promptly marched back to Prestonburg wasn't a way he wanted to tempt fate. In fact, Eddie figured they'd strap a parachute to his back and push him out over Prestonburg just to cut down on red tape.

He'd have to start clean, from the beginning. And of course Vickie needed a passport, too. Eddie knew just the right person to ask for help.

Jason Pine had offered Eddie his services a few months before Eddie had gone off to do his time at

Prestonburg. He'd met Pine when a mutual friend had referred him to Eddie. Pine had asked him to make some ATM cards using data he'd retrieved from bank records that were supposed to have been shredded but weren't. Eddie appreciated the business, but it made him nervous whenever he got a referral. He didn't necessarily consider referrals in his business as a good thing. He knew it was just as likely that a referral could be a guy in a cheap suit with a badge pinned to the inside pocket.

Eddie hadn't needed a fake passport at the time as he had a perfectly good one from Great Britain. Although the price that Pine asked was reasonable, Eddie figured the real thing was better than anything Pine would make, although he later heard that Pine was regarded as a real craftsman.

Pine ran a small specialty printing business in the Bronx and *supplemented* his income when business got slow in the shop. Pine was able to provide his clients who had enough cash with driver's licenses, passports, or enough impressive diplomas and certificates to fill a waiting room wall.

Eddie hadn't seen Pine in over four years. He hoped that Pine was still there and not himself a guest of New York's penal system. He'd also need a lot more cash and he'd need a couple of credit cards. He had no problem using ATM cards of his own manufacture. If the ATM rejected his card, he could simply walk away. If a credit card of his own making was rejected, he would have to try to explain it to a live person – a someone who might not like his explanation.

Eddie preferred to use the prepaid cards where there would be no such problem. Eddie didn't like confrontation. While Vickie was pouting, he thought it would be a good time to take a few cards and hit some ATMs.

He was back within an hour and a half and was over five thousand dollars richer. He hadn't been back in the apartment for a couple of minutes when the bedroom door slowly opened again and a surprisingly pretty woman eased through the door. She was dressed in a chic pair of black slacks and a stylish red silk blouse. Matching belt and closed toe pumps finished the ensemble. Before Eddie could ask "Where's Vickie?" he caught himself and said, "Wow!"

"I'm sorry, Eddie." She said as demurely as she could, lower lip turned down in a submissive look. "I'm hungry."

Eddie laughed. "You don't want to go out to dinner with a guy looking like me. Give me a couple of minutes."

Over dinner he'd explain his plan to Vickie and tomorrow he'd take the train to the Bronx and get the next step started. He'd make a visit to Jason Pine and his specialty printing shop.

Chapter Five

The Bronx

Eddie knew he'd have to keep her occupied while he was gone to see Pine, so he gave gave Vickie the assignment of going out and buying luggage for both of them. It had been long enough since he had been to Pine's neighborhood in the Bronx that he'd forgotten how many transfers he'd need to make on the MTA. He thought it was at least three so he'd be gone for several hours. Vickie's initial excitement at the idea of going to England was now replaced by a case of jitters that Eddy hadn't seen in her before.

When she had asked how they were getting to England, he quickly answered that they would be flying of course and almost followed that with "what kind of a stupid question is that?"

He quickly caught himself when he saw the flare of fear show in her widened eyes. And there was something about that crazy salamander that made him cautious. It seemed to move whenever Vickie's fuse was getting short.

Eddie was relieved when he exited the Castle Hill MTA station in the Bronx and found the neighborhood looked the same as it had when he was there last – seedy looking and a place you wouldn't want to hang around after dark. But Eddie had no plans to be there any longer than necessary. He had no problems finding Pine's hole-in-the-wall print shop tucked in between a chain sandwich shop and a tattoo parlor.

Pine was pretty much the same, too, except that he was now sporting tattoos covering both arms.

Apparently he was spending a lot of time and money with his next door neighbor. Pine's was one of those shops that had a little bell attached to the front door that tinkled whenever it was opened. Pine didn't even look up as Eddie came in and approached the desk where he was busily absorbed in his work.

"Hello, Jason. It's been a long time." Eddie said as he stood directly in front of Pine. Pine jumped and raked something from the top of the desk where he was working into a drawer and drove it closed with his stomach. He slid forward in his chair.

"Eddie Fairfax, is that really you?" Pine grinned and held out his hand. "I thought you were . . .

"I was," Eddie cut him off, "but that's history and now I need a favor. You still doing passports?"

Pine's eyes narrowed and he glanced over Eddie's shoulder toward the shop's door. "Depends," he said as one hand was slowly pushing something else out of Eddie's sight.

"Depends" Eddie asked, "on what?"

"Well, a guy I haven't seen in years shows up asking real serious questions about my business. No hellos, no how's it going? No chit chat! I don't even know what you're doing now. Maybe they made a snitch out of you." Pine's face showed a wariness that Eddie understood.

"Sorry, man. I guess my social skills are a little rusty. Yeah, I've been back for a few weeks and thought I'd take my girl friend down to Mexico for a little R&R." Then Eddie grinned, "Me, a snitch? That's real funny." Pine's shoulders relaxed a little and the wary look began to fade. He quickly put on his customer service persona. "Yeah, I'm still doing 'um. When do you need them?"

"As soon as you can have them," Eddie said hopefully.

Pine decided to test the market a bit, "It'll be a grand for the pair, but they'll look just like the real thing, real numbers and all." He waited for Eddie's reaction. "I'll even put a couple of stamps in'um if you want. Makes 'em look better. Then you just have to bend 'em up a bit. Make 'em, look used."

Eddie held Pine's expectant stare but decided not to negotiate. "When?"

"Three days, if you've got pictures."

Eddie laid the 2 inch by 2 inch shots of Vickie and himself on Pine's desk. Pine snatched them up and adjusted his glasses as he looked at Vickie's picture. "You didn't waste any time. She's a looker." Then Pine squinted and held the picture closer, "What the hell's that on her neck?"

Eddie ignored Pines's last remark and said, "Thanks". He spent a few minutes giving Pine some reasonable information for the ID page and then said, "See you in three days." He heard the tinkle of the little bell as the door closed behind him. He thought about finding an ATM to make his trip more efficient and productive since he hadn't expected the passports to cost a thousand dollars.

He guessed that it was just the effects of inflation while he'd been living upstate for the last four years. Not seeing anything that looked like an ATM anywhere nearby, he decided that the risk of getting mugged in Pine's neighborhood was better than average and headed back to Manhattan.

Over the next three days Eddie continued to amass a horde of cash. The judge finally put a stop to Eddie's hits on his account but not before Eddie had exacted a satisfying measure of revenge. Eddie even used his new software to worm through to another of the judge's accounts and clean it out. Vickie was busy arranging and re-arranging and trying new colors of matching polish for her fingers and toes. She had also forgotten to shop for luggage. "I'm sorry, Eddie, I'll go tomorrow and buy some."

"That's ok," Eddie said, "I'll get it when I go back to Pine's place." He wondered what kind of luggage she would have brought home had she remembered to buy some. Vickie offered no argument and returned to folding and unfolding clothes.

Eddie wanted to avoid any problems with his probation officer, waiting until after his monthly check-in to leave. He emailed the solicitor that he would arrive in Gloucestershire on Monday, May 11. The solicitor responded that the reading of the will would take place immediately. Actually, Eddie wanted to arrive a couple of days early just for last minute strategy and in case the airlines had delays. He bought two tickets on British Airways flight 6137 for Saturday from JFK to London Heathrow.

He waited for Pine's requested three days and took the train back to the Bronx to pick up their passports. When Eddie opened Pine's shop door he gave the little bell a few extra jiggles. As was the case with his previous visit, Eddie was the only customer in the store. He thought about trying to negotiate the price down from a grand but remembered that Pine had a quick temper and decided that saving the judge a hundred or two wasn't worth making Pine angry.

Pine heard the bell this time and looked up to see Eddie coming in. Eddie hadn't wanted to surprise him again. That might be dangerous. Pine put on his customer service smile and came from behind the counter.

"Eddie, how's it going?"

"Ok, I guess." Eddie kept a straight face and reluctantly took Pine's outstretched hand. He didn't want to get too friendly and have Pine asking too many questions. Just get the passports and get out. It was better that way.

Pine knew that most people who bought his passports weren't usually going on pleasure trips and he had an unusually strong curiosity about what people were using them for. He was also smart enough to realize that Eddie seemed to be in a hurry and wasn't going to stay around for small talk. He didn't care. Eddie hadn't tried to negotiate and at the price he quoted it was a very profitable transaction. Pine opened his top desk drawer and withdrew the two documents and handed them to Eddie.

"Whadda ya think? First class, huh? Probably the best I've ever made."

"Yeah, looks great."

Eddie laid his on the counter and opened Vickie's to the ID page. The picture looked authentic, the number looked genuine and the name jumped at him like a jack-in-the-box. "What the hell is this? *Victoria Fairfax*! Where'd you come up with that?" Eddie's voice had ratcheted up a notch.

"You forgot to tell me her last name, or at least if you did, I didn't get it written down. Actually traveling as husband and wife is safer at passport control," Pine said helpfully. "And I knew you were in a hurry."

"She's not my wife."

"Well, I know that and you know that but . . ."

"Forget it," Eddie said, as he pulled a roll of bills from his pocket and counted out a thousand dollars to Pine, "We'll make it work."

Eddie slipped the passports into his pocket and turned to go. After a couple of steps, it occurred to him that he should probably leave Pine on a friendly basis and looked back to say 'so long' or 'goodbye' or something. Pine was already holding the hundred dollar bills up to a light and squinting at each one through a magnifying glass. Same to you, Eddie thought and gave the shop door a harder slam than was necessary and heard the satisfying rattle of the glass. He grinned and felt he understood Vickie's penchant for door slamming a little bit. Might even be considered therapeutic.

On second thought, he hoped Vickie wouldn't start slamming their door when she looked at her passport. After all, she had said her name was 'just Vickie' when he'd asked her and a passport needed at least two names. He was reasonably sure that Cher, Pink, and Madonna had last names on their passports.

When he returned to the apartment, Vickie was in the process of repacking for the hundredth time she said. Her clothes were all over the bedroom and had started to spill over into the living room. The green 'St. Patrick Day' slacks she loved so much were draped over the back of his plastic lawn chair.

"Can I see my passport?" She beamed.

Eddie pulled the small blue-covered book from his pocket and laid it in her hand. She flipped it open to the picture page and read for several seconds. Eddie waited. Would she throw it down and go into a pout or would she even notice?

Vickie looked up at him with eyebrows raised, "So . . . I'm Victoria Fairfax?"

"Well, you needed a last name."

She considered the document for a few seconds and began to smile. "I'm cool with that." she said.

Vickie returned to the bedroom for what Eddie figured would be more packing. He could pack a lot quicker, he knew, and he'd do it later. He dropped into the old lawn chair and booted up the computer. He wanted to check in with Edward's email again. If there was anything else from the solicitor, he needed to catch it before Edward saw it. He realized he wasn't concentrating as well as usual because he knew when she left. Usually, he never realized she was gone until she knocked on the door when she returned but today she had playfully nibbled at his ear before scooting out the door. It was an automatic locking door and she often forgot her key. She was usually gone several hours but today she was back early. He glanced at his watch when he heard her knock and saw that she had been gone barely an hour. "Coming," he called as he pushed back the chair. He wondered if something was wrong.

Eddie pulled the door open to let her in and was startled to find two squarely built men in dark suits filling up the corridor where Vickie was usually waiting. They had to be from the black sedan across the street, he was sure. Eddie's could practically hear his pulse begin to rev up.

"Eddie Fairfax?" the nearer of the two said his name like a question. He flipped open a leather wallet to reveal a NYPD shield. "We'd like to talk to you." They didn't wait for Eddie's invitation but pushed past him into the living room. Eddie had to think fast. His thoughts started flashing back to Prestonburg. What was going on? Had he made some stupid mistake again? Had he missed something crucial? How had he been careless this time?

He was watching their faces and could practically feel their contempt as they took in the apartment and its tired, threadbare look.

"We've been talking to a friend of yours," said the other cop. "We've been watching his little shop in the Bronx."

Damn, thought Eddie, Jason Pine had turned him in. But why? He'd never done anything to Pine but pay him an exorbitant price for the two passports.

Shit, that was it, he thought. They knew about the passports. His rotten luck was starting all over again.

The first cop, shorter and built like a bulldog with wide shoulders and a chest way too big for his suit jacket, had walked over to Eddie's computer and stood staring at the screen. "What were you doing at Pine's place," he asked casually as his eyes flicked about the screen. Eddie stalled and asked, "I'm sorry, what did you say?" The cop at the computer continued staring at the screen without answering. Eddie prayed that he knew nothing about computer code. The officer nearer Eddie, a head taller than his partner, answered for him. "He asked what you were doing at Jason Pine's place. Pine said you owed him some money and came in to pay up. That true?"

Eddie stuffed his hands deep into his pockets. They always shook when he was nervous. "Yeah, that's right. I owed him some money."

"It just seemed a little odd to us that an ex-con still on probation suddenly needed to go all the way to the Bronx right after a four year stint upstate." The cop's accusation hung in the air like stale smoke that wouldn't float away but Eddie had learned another valuable lesson at Prestonburg – don't answer questions that aren't questions. "How much did you owe him, anyway?" The cop was now getting direct and it was a question he'd have to answer.

Eddie tried to keep a calm face and hoped that his answer matched Pine's. "It was a grand," Eddie finally said. "I'm trying to make a clean start and just thought I needed to take care of some debts." Eddie waited while the tall one scribbled his answer in a little notebook and then looked up. He did the cop thing with his eyes as if he were x-raying Eddie, "That's right big of you, Fairfax. Any more debts you need to settle?" Eddie shrugged and looked out of the corner of his eye at the bulldog who was still fixated on his computer.

No, he groaned inwardly, he must be able to read code. The tall one flipped the cover of his notepad closed, "so how did you come up with a grand so fast?" Eddie saw that the bulldog had finally turned around and was looking at him too. Both waited for his answer. This had to be the trick question, Eddie thought. Always a trick question.

"You seem to know everything about me, so yeah, I was upstate for four years. I saved every penny I made," Eddie said, and then added, "Not much to spend it on up there."

That seemed to satisfy the bulldog for a few seconds but then he jerked a thumb in the direction of Eddie's computer, "What's this?" The screen glowed accusingly. Eddie knew this was the one answer he absolutely had to get right or they'd be slapping cuffs on him before he could get finished with the wrong one.

"It's software code. It's my job now. I do freelance work setting up websites for small businesses." That was partly true. Eddie had almost turned down a small job for an old acquaintance who wanted a website for his catering business. Eddie hated that kind of work and only agreed to do it to return a favor and now he was so thankful that he had. "I'll show you, he said." He quickly stepped between the bulldog and his computer and sat down in the lawn chair. With a few keystrokes he pulled up the half-finished website for Baker Street

Catering. "There," he said, "That's what I do now." Both cops peered at the screen and the notebook came back out and the tall one started scribbling again.

"That's impressive," the bulldog said. "I wish I understood that stuff."

"Just a word of advice," said the tall cop after he had put his notebook away again, "stay away from Pine."

"And don't screw up," said the bulldog. "You've got a check-in with your parole officer on the fifth. You wouldn't want to miss it. A lot of guys start off ok after getting out but pretty soon get lazy and forget about their parole rules. Don't let that happen with you. Could mean a trip back upstate." Both the bulldog and the scribbler turned to go but the bulldog wheeled around, nose to nose with Eddie, "Another thing," he said . . .

Eddie tensed, expecting to hear the real reason they'd come. . .he was going to ask to see the passports . . . "be sure and report to your parole officer that we've talked," the bulldog said instead. "Any contact you have with law enforcement has to be reported."

Eddie was about to thank the cop for his concern when that familiar knock came at the door. Shit, Eddie thought, not now . . . not yet. Why did she have to come home now? She'll probably tell them everything about their plans for England and a dozen other wrong answers. He had gotten so close to getting them out the door and now he was definitely screwed. They wouldn't stand there and listen to her knock forever. Shit, he said to himself again, just another five minutes. That's all he would have needed.

He took a deep breath and decided he might as well get the inevitable over with. He pulled the door open.

Vickie waited in her usual spot and at first seemed surprised at finding two strangers standing in their living room. Before Eddie could say anything he noticed the salamander begin to pulsate along her jugular. She looked from one cop to the other and finally at Eddie, her eyes narrowed and her lips tightened, "I'm still furious with you." She stormed past the three of them and at the bedroom door turned around and eyed the cops again. Then she glared at Eddie and stamped her foot, "No, I'm not furious. . . I'm mad as hell." She spun around, charged through the door and gave it a slam that rattled that morning's dirty dishes in the nearby sink. Eddie tried a weak grin on the cops, "We had a little disagreement this morning."

"She'll get over it," said the bulldog with a little grin as he headed for the door. "They always do."

The scribbler grinned too, "Go buy her some flowers."

Yeah, right, thought Eddie.

When the door was finally closed, Eddie slumped in his chair. He felt like he had been beaten. His pulse was racing at full speed and sweat trickled down his forehead. He looked back at the words glowing on the computer's screen – Baker Street Catering, and said another prayer of thanks.

The bedroom door quietly opened and Vickie slipped out, looking around the living room. "What were the cops doing here?" she asked.

Eddie had his own question. "How did you know they were cops?" he said, surprised.

"The smell," she said with distaste and went back through the door.

Chapter Six

JFK Airport, NYC

Eddie had to admit that traveling by air had changed a bit since he had come to America six years before and none of the changes were for the better, but he hadn't expected as much. What he hadn't counted on was the anxiety of getting Vickie through the intricacies of airport security. It was her first time to fly and undergo the searches taken for granted by most air travelers. He had to intervene and explain to TSA agents that she didn't mean everything she said and he was sweating profusely by the time he finally got her to the departure gate. She had barely escaped being detained by a quartet of gruff agents who would have declared her a security risk had they not been so amused.

Eddie found two seats together at the gate and, glancing at his watch, saw that they had a half-hour before boarding was to begin. Vickie was still very tense from her pat-downs and was looking around the gate area as if she expected even more personal searches to occur. The salamander actually appeared to be quivering as if about to spring out of her shirt. Finally, she settled down and remembered more basic needs, "Eddie, where's the bathroom? And I'm hungry."

"The restrooms are down that concourse," he said, pointing toward the way they had just come. "But there isn't time to get food. There's food on the plane. We'll be boarding soon, so hurry back."

Vickie said nothing but grabbed her purse and headed in the direction Eddie had indicated. Eddie moved to two seats nearer the gate desk and quickly became engrossed with his new laptop computer. It was one of his last purchases before leaving for England. He realized he'd need internet access to keep tabs on Edward and his email and to intercept any further communication from the solicitor.

He also checked on train schedules from Heathrow to Paddington Station in London and on to Gloucestershire. He had an amazing power to concentrate when he was at the computer keyboard and missed hearing the boarding call. He finally noticed all the activity around him, saw that a line had already formed and turned to tell Vickie that they were ready to board.

The seat to his left was empty except for her carry-on bag. He looked around to see if she was in line but there was no Vickie anywhere at the gate. Eddie felt a flush of panic. He gathered up his computer, returned it to its case, and grabbed the other things they were carrying aboard.

He hurried to the concourse and looked both ways. There was no henna-red hair in either direction. He looked at the boarding line that was now beginning to snake into the jetway. He approached the gate agent and explained that his *wife* had gone to the restroom – he stopped to look at his watch and was shocked when he saw how long it had been – she had been gone almost forty minutes. The agent agreed to page Vickie but beyond that said nothing could be done.

Eddie cringed when he heard the announcement.

"Passenger Victoria Fairfax, please proceed to gate B22, your flight is in the process of boarding. If you do not report to the gate for immediate boarding your bags will be off-loaded and your reservation cancelled."

Jeez, Vickie, where are you, he thought. He could just imagine her response when she heard that announcement. He waited by the jetway door and paced as he watched the final passenger in the boarding line disappear around the far corner. He looked hopefully at the agent who was busy on the phone probably telling the pilot that some crazy guy was still standing at the gate trying to decide what to do. "Sir, I'm afraid we can wait no longer. You'll have to proceed alone or take a later flight."

He looked back toward the concourse. There were hundreds of people streaming by, but no bright henna hair, no Vickie.

He had to make a decision.

If he didn't take this flight what would happen to their bags thousands of miles away in London if they weren't there to claim them? There were several thousand dollars in cash in his and since they were traveling on false passports, he sure didn't want to raise their profile by filing claims for lost luggage. He didn't want to do anything out of the ordinary. More importantly, when he didn't keep his appointment at the solicitor's office on Monday, the solicitor would likely try to email Edward and he might not be able to intercept it. Edward would know what he knew, and he wasn't ready for that. In vain, he searched the sea of faces in the concourse one more time.

She wasn't there.

He turned and handed his boarding pass to the gate agent.

Eddie found his seat and pushed his computer bag and Vickie's carry-on under the seats in front of theirs. He closed his eyes and tried to think what had happened. Where had she gone? Fortunately, he had given her a couple of hundred dollars so he knew she could get a cab back to the apartment, that is, if she could think her problem through to that solution.

He knew she was going to be angry but he hoped that she didn't panic. What was so hard about walking a few steps down the concourse to the ladies' restroom? He was feeling terrible about leaving her but he knew he had made the right decision. It had to be done. Edward couldn't find out about his inheritance before Eddie had a chance to see what it was all about.

He had just about convinced himself that he was right and that she would be ok when a sharp blow

connected to his left ribs. His eyes popped open to confront a furious face that was almost the same color as
the henna hair. A skinny elbow still pushed hard against
his side.

"Eddie, were you trying to leave me?" She was now
digging her nails into his left arm.

"What happened to you?' he gasped. "I waited and
waited. Where were you?"

"I was hungry," she said as she pulled a bag of chips
from her purse. Her anger melted away quicker than the
pain in his ribs. "I got lost and couldn't remember which
gate we were at."

Eddie closed his eyes and dropped his chin to his
chest. He was suddenly very tired. When he heard the
crunching of chips, he turned back to her and asked,
"How did you finally find it?"

"Find what?"

"The gate," he said, exasperated.

"I heard them call my name – my new name." She
grinned. "That was cool."

The jet's huge engines began to roar and both were
pushed back in their seats. Eddie had never been a fan
of flying and closed his eyes as the big Boeing accelerated down the runway like a mad, charging elephant.
He had a firm grip on both armrests and held on until
he was sure the plane had achieved a few thousand feet
of altitude. He hated the takeoff part and remembered
Vickie's wild look when he had first mentioned flying.
He hoped she wouldn't panic and make a scene.

He finally opened his eyes and turned to see how
she was doing. The empty chip bag sat propped on her
lap and she was snoring at a level just loud enough to

hear over the whine of the jet's engines. He smiled at the funny scene. If Vickie had a calling card, he thought amazed, it would undoubtedly read, *Just Vickie, sleep anywhere. . . always hungry.* What else could she possibly add, he wondered, as he recalled her quickness with a story when the two cops had him thoroughly rattled. And the fact that she immediately sensed who they were . . .

Eddie closed his eyes and drifted to sleep. He dreamed about seeing England again for the first time in years.

Chapter Seven

Heathrow Airport, London

Both Eddie and Vickie were awakened by the flight attendant tapping them on the shoulder. It was time to raise their seatbacks, she said, they were landing.

Vickie squinted at him. "You said they'd have food on the plane. I'm really starving."

"Don't worry," he said, "you wouldn't have liked it. Anyway, we'll get some breakfast after we get through customs and get our bags."

"What's customs," she asked.

Getting through customs with fake passports was something that had worried Eddie and now that they were closer to actually doing it, he was more than worried. No one paid that much attention when you were leaving a country, but coming in, it got a little stickier. He'd have to work hard at not being nervous.

Like most cops, Eddie was sure the customs people could smell fear on a person like a cheap cologne. He'd heard that Jason Pine did top quality work. He took a deep breath and hoped it was true.

He tried to sound calmer than he actually was. "It's where you show them your passport and they put a little stamp on it as a souvenir."

Vickie leaned forward and looked out the window as the plane taxied toward the gate. "I thought England would look a lot different." She sounded disappointed. "And it's raining."

Eddie shook his head. "It's an airport. They all look alike. And it's England. It rains a lot. It'll look different when we get on the train."

Their plane had arrived at a lull in traffic and they were going to get through customs quickly. Eddie was beginning to relax and believe everything would go smoothly. They had worked their way through the queue and were finally standing at the yellow line waiting for the customs agent to motion them forward. Eddie just hoped that she wouldn't ask the customs agent where there was a good restaurant. A uniform with cropped hair and a government attitude finally gave a curt wave.

Eddie smiled and handed the man their passports. The agent opened the first one and looked at Eddie. Eddie smiled again. The agent looked from the passport to Eddie and back to the passport. He flipped through several pages and finally slammed down the stamp machine like Eddie's passport was a giant insect he had to kill and handed it back.

Eddie was just starting to breathe easier when the agent asked Vickie why she was coming to England. She got a puzzled look on her face and looked at Eddie. "Jeez, I don't know. Why are we coming to England, Eddie?"

Unable to pull off a David Copperfield-style disappearance, Eddie quickly tried humor. "Quit kidding, Vickie." He turned back to the customs man, "We're on our honeymoon." Then he tried his biggest, goofiest grin on the agent. "She's a lot prettier in person than in her picture, ain't she?"

Eddie's heart was pounding as he waited. The agent's face said he hated anybody with an attitude and especially anybody who tried to be funny. Eddie figured the agent also hated tattoos. He could feel all his plans coming unglued and a brief, ugly image of Prestonburg flashed through his mind. The agent continued to stare at Eddie, drilling holes with his eyes. Finally his hand began to move and Eddie was sure it was reaching for a gun. They were going to be arrested on the spot.

Eddie was just about to run when the agent brought the stamp down on Vickie's passport with a thud that must have shaken the entire booth. Eddie was relieved when Vickie reached out to take the passport from the agent. His own hand was shaking so badly he had to stuff it in his pocket. He felt sure the agent could see it.

Eddie's hands were still twitching as he led Vickie into a Caffe Nero. He planned to say something about the near fiasco at customs, but not before feeding her. He'd learned a lot about her priorities and knew she didn't do well when she was hungry, and she hadn't eaten for hours. She was probably nearing some kind of flashpoint.

As he sat and watched her consume a couple of bagels and some sort of chocolate pastry, he was having second thoughts.

A shiver ran up his spine as he thought what would have happened if she had told the customs agent the truth. 'We're here to check out a guy's inheritance. Eddie found out about it by hacking his email.' He doubted they could have laughed their way out of that one.

"You did a great job back there." he told her. And that was true considering most of the alternatives Eddie could think of.

"Aren't you going to eat anything?" she asked as she munched through the last bite of chocolate thing.

"No, I kinda lost my appetite." he said. "Can you wait here for a couple of minutes while I find an ATM?"

"Why, you've already got a ton of money and . . ."

"I need to get some pounds." He saw the confused look on her face. "It's the money they use here in England."

"Oh, ok."

"Can you wait right here and watch the bags?" She nodded as she wiped a glob of chocolate from her lip.

Eddie left her and headed straight for an ATM he remembered passing as they were looking for a breakfast place. He had made several new cards to use on the trip. As much as he would like for the judge to finance the trip, he didn't want any electronic connections between the judge and England, something he wouldn't want to explain later if it ever came to that. After taking a substantial amount from the ATM, he decided to expand his options and exchanged a couple of thousand dollars for pounds at a nearby currency exchange kiosk.

Eddie was feeling good about the trip after the scare at customs. He stopped at a small shop and bought Vickie a little bottle of perfume. He figured it would probably be her first. He went back into the Caffe Nero and turned toward the back corner where Vickie was waiting.

"Damn!" He froze in his tracks and looked back to the front. Yes, it was the right place! He even recognized the grossly overweight man at a nearby table, still busily shoving food into his mouth.

Vickie was gone. Their bags were gone. He hurried to the table where he had left her only minutes before. The empty plate and cup, still on the table, wadded napkin with smears of chocolate. Then he noticed their bags laying flat on the floor and pushed under a bench. He practically fell on his knees and zipped open a pocket on the side of his piece of luggage. Thrusting his hand into the pocket he felt the comforting bulk of several thousand dollars filling up the whole compartment. Now he could relax . . . and be pissed!

"What are you doing?" he heard Vickie say, indifferently, behind him.

He stood and pulled the bags upright and gave both an unmistakable drop on their bottoms. Vickie winced. Eddie gritted his teeth. "Where have you been? You can't just leave stuff not being watched and expect it to be here when you get back." He dropped his voice and leaned closer. He wanted her to feel his anger. "Most of the money was in that bag and you left it and took off somewhere."

"I had to pee. I hadn't been to the ladies' since New York."

He felt like shouting at her, but what good would it do, he decided. She was going to be a liability.

"Let's go," he said sharply to her and motioned her toward the door. He followed, pulling both bags. He was going to watch them himself. He stopped just before the door, reached into his pocket, pulled out the bag with the bottle of perfume and dropped it in the trash.

Chapter Eight

Train - London to Gloucester

The train ride to Paddington Station passed in silence. Vickie stared out the window with her chin propped on her palm, watching the seedy suburbs of London appear and disappear in the grey mist. Eddie's mood was in sync with the weather, but he knew if he said anything to her, he'd probably regret it later. It was just easier to look after things himself.

He had taken the big bundle of US dollars out of the luggage and divided it between the pockets of his jacket and pants. He still kept a sharp eye on the bags. By the time they were on the train out of Paddington toward Gloucestershire, Vickie's mood had begun to thaw and he had begun to really appreciate the salamander. It was proving to be a good indicator of what was going on inside her head, and Eddie needed all the help he could get in that area.

Although both were city people, at least Eddie had recently lived in the country. Unfortunately, his full exposure to the delights of nature had been limited to viewing them through the grimy windows of a prison bus. Vickie had never seen so much open space before and was taken in by the strange world outside the train's window.

The rain had finally stopped somewhere west of the town of High Wycombe and a thin, watery sunlight began to take some of the soggy look out of the landscape. The drab tenements surrounding the train line had finally given way to green, rolling hills dotted here and there by clumps of wet animals huddling against the weather. Vickie gave a little squeal and pointed out the window. "Is that a cow?" she asked, giggling.

Eddie noticed that several other passengers were now staring at Vickie and starting to smile. "I don't think so," he said, "and keep it down a bit, ok?"

Eddie was beginning to realize that Vickie was not just unpredictable but he wasn't going to be able to depend on her. She always gave in to her two main impulses – eating, sleeping, and now, a third one, going to the 'ladies.' Within twelve hours, she had gotten lost and almost missed the flight, abandoned their bags, and had pouted when she wasn't sleeping or eating. He'd see what happened through the rest of the weekend. While she remained focused on the countryside flying by, he was trying to imagine what his appointment with solicitor Rhetts was going to be like on Wednesday.

He'd already decided that he couldn't take Vickie, but what to do with her while he was busy with Rhetts was a question he had no answer for. If the last few hours were any indication, she could probably either get lost or find some other way to complicate things. He thought of not staying in Gloucester but going on to the little town of Moreton-in-Marsh where Rhetts had his office. She might get temporarily misplaced, but certainly not get lost. He'd wait to decide that when they got to Gloucester. In a moment of black humor, he thought that he knew what she was doing in New York when she would leave the apartment and be gone for the day. She was getting lost in the first few minutes and spending the rest of the day finding her way back.

The idea of the Wednesday meeting was all new to him, but he had always been good at 'flying by the seat of his pants.' He wondered if the solicitor was a suspicious sort. He worried about the process of going through a will. What could it tell him about Edward that he didn't already know, that he needed to know? And how much did the solicitor know about Edward?

Fortunately, Eddie felt that he knew Edward well enough to carry on a reasonable conversation with the solicitor. And then there might come the time when he took what he learned from the solicitor and actually confronted Edward. After all, Edward had betrayed him once – a betrayal that had cost him four years of his life. He didn't know why, but he still expected that Edward owed him something special. Perhaps Edward had completely misunderstood their connection or even been pressured into his damning testimony.

He was sure Edward's response this time would be more favorable. Their common burden would affect Edward's response, and of course, Edward had had four years to think about their last encounter . . . and Eddie vaguely heard Edward calling his name. An elbow connected to his right ribs this time. It was Vickie calling his name. He turned to her, almost surprised that it hadn't been Edward saying his name.

"What?" he asked.

"What's wrong with you? What are you going to do?" she asked

"About what?" He wasn't sure how she had gotten into his thoughts about Edward.

"What are you going to do about his inheritance? Are you going to take it?"

"I . . ." He hadn't actually thought about it that way. It had all been about a connection with Edward, an answer that told him something important about himself. He knew, too, that there were some thoughts about revenge that got mixed up with his other thoughts about Edward. He almost loved Edward like a brother, but brothers still knew how to hurt you. And Vickie . . . she kept looking at him expecting him to say something he wasn't prepared to talk about, something he hadn't even thought that much about.

"Are you going to take his inheritance?" she repeated.

"I don't know. I don't even know what it is yet."

"You came all this way just because you're curious?"

"Yes . . . I mean . . no!" Eddie wasn't prepared to debate with Vickie. "I'll have an idea after I talk to the solicitor."

After all, that's why he had come to England. This man was the key to finding out more about Edward. When he had more information, then he could decide what to do. With all the screw-ups, he didn't think Vickie had any right to ask so many questions.

"I'll tell you after I see the solicitor."

"You're not taking me with you?" She turned in her seat, her voice rising.

"Keep it down, I told you." Eddie stole a glance at the salamander.

Vickie grunted, crossed her arms and turned back to the window. Some fellow passengers were still watching and that made him nervous. "Ok, let's get to Gloucestershire, find a hotel and get something to eat. Then we'll talk about it."

Chapter Eight

Moreton-in-Marsh, Gloucestershire

Eddie and Vickie checked in at the Redesdale Arms Hotel near the Moreton-in-Marsh train station and spent the weekend resting from the strains of the trip and trying to recover from jet lag. Vickie was returning to her carefree, easygoing self until Eddie insisted on finding the solicitor's office before the Wednesday appointment. He wanted to be sure he knew where it was so that he wouldn't be late Wednesday. He also wanted to see the neighborhood and have a day or two to get familiar with the place. That might help prepare him for his meeting with Solicitor Rhetts and reveal something about Edward.

It also reminded Vickie that he wasn't planning to take her to the meeting and set off another argument. Although she was quick to take exception to Eddie's plans whenever they didn't agree with hers, she had little stamina for a drawn-out fight. She gave in when Eddie bought her a big assortment of nail polish at the Tuesday market and suggested that she use the time while he was away at the meeting to give herself a manicure and a pedicure. He'd fill her in on all that he learned when he returned.

On Wednesday morning, Vickie lay with the blanket tucked under her chin. Breathing easily, she twitched and made small satisfied sleeping noises that Eddie took to be dreams about the ten little bottles of nail polish lined up toy-soldier fashion on her night table, ready to do duty, one after the other. Hopefully, they would keep her occupied while he got to know Solicitor Rhetts.

Eddie quietly slipped from the room, out of the hotel and turned toward the small side street where he had an appointment with a Claiborne Rhetts of Dunham Solicitors at ten o'clock.

The offices of Dunham Solicitors at number 13 New Road was in a building that had seen better times. Eddie wasn't surprised. If their practice depended on the reading of wills for what Eddie presumed to be the working class, then a trendy glass and steel box in a fancy neighborhood wasn't to be expected. If the looks of the place didn't speak to lawyerly prosperity, at least it was convenient, only a few blocks from the hotel.

He stopped for a coffee to fortify his nerves and a last minute review of his strategy. Actually, he didn't have a strategy. He had little idea of what the reading of a will entailed in general and what it might mean for him in particular. He didn't know what, if anything, was expected of him, and he sure had no clue as to what he should expect from the solicitor.

He stopped for a moment when he realized how he was thinking; he was thinking as if he were Edward. He'd never impersonated anyone before, he'd always been anonymous in what he did, took what he wanted at arm's length. But this had to be the next step forward, he told himself, this was where he was going to find the answer. He, Eddie, would have to convincingly play the part of Edward.

Was his meeting with Rhetts to be ten minutes and out or was he going to be there for hours? He just hoped that finding out who was close enough to Edward to leave him something in a will would bring him closer to an answer. Before Edward had come along, Eddie had worried that he might have found the answer to his problem but hadn't recognized it, that it had been there for the taking, and yet he had let it slip by unknown, unaware.

Finding Edward had been a catalyst to his thinking – if he was ever to find a solution, he had to know exactly what the problem was, and since Edward had apparently succeeded where he had so far failed, it was obvious that Edward knew exactly what to look for. It was imperative to know everything Edward knew.

Eddie asked himself again if he was making too big an issue of his name and its problems. No, he shook his head to himself. No! It *was* an issue, an important one. Edward had apparently worked through it, and with his help, Eddie could too. Their little courtroom confrontation four years before had been an aberration, something spurred on by lawyers. With hindsight, Edward would be able to see that he had been unfair, too harsh with someone who could benefit from his own experience, someone who needed his help to get through troubles he had already overcome.

Eddie stopped on the narrow sidewalk in front of the two story building and glanced at his wrist, it was time. He pushed the glass door open and stepped into a lobby that looked like it should belong in Jason Pine's neighborhood. Eddie had the feeling that he might be the first client to pass through in days or weeks. It had the dusty, musty smell of age.

He mounted the double-back set of stairs and stopped in front of suite 2278. He looked again at the copy of the email he had just pulled from his pocket for the hundredth time. The number was right. A longer number than necessary, he thought, to distinguish the offices of Dunham Solicitors from only other two doors he could see on the short hallway. He turned the knob and pushed the door open to find himself staring at a large desk, stacked high with disorderly piles of dusty documents and presided over by an empty chair.

Eddie walked closer to the desk and peered over it at the chair as if he expected to find some diminutive secretary waiting on Claiborne Rhetts' callers. The chair had a fine covering of dust like that on the stacks of papers. Nobody had sat there for some time. In fact, it looked as if no one had been in the room at all in recent weeks or months. The ceilings were high and marred with water stains and draped with cobwebs. Totally absent were all indications of a modern office – no phone or calculator, no tangle of wires running from one device to another. It was an office from another generation.

"Hello," Eddie called. His voice echoed off the bare walls. He heard drawers being slammed shut behind the door on his left. Eddie concentrated on the door for several seconds and was about to knock when the door slowly creaked open. An ancient figure slipped through. The man must be at least eighty, Eddie thought. The old man adjusted some wireframe glasses on a long, bony nose and looked Eddie up and down. "You must be Fairfax," he said with a faint hint of annoyance. "I'm Rhetts."

"Yeah, I'm Eddie . . . uh, Edward . . . Fairfax." Eddie stuck out his hand. The old man looked at it as if he were going to read Eddie's palm, decided he wasn't interested, and ignored it. He dusted off the chair with a well used handkerchief he pulled from pants that shined in the seat from eons of wear. "I'm Rhetts," he said again as he dropped into the chair. A small whiff of dust accompanied his movement. "Pull up that chair over there," he pointed with a crooked finger at a rickety chair that Eddie hadn't noticed because it, too, was stacked high with old files.

Once Eddie had positioned his chair in front of Rhetts' desk, he sat down and waited. This wasn't exactly what he had envisioned during the hours and hours he had thought about this very moment.

Rhetts adjusted a few of the papers giving the impression there was a definite order to the reading of a will. Eddie waited, encouraged. Finally, getting things organized to his satisfaction, the old man crossed thin, veiny hands between stacks of clutter on the desk. He stared at Eddie as if unable to decide exactly where to begin. At last, he found his starting point.

"I'm glad he's dead," Rhetts said.

"Excuse me, Eddie managed to say, not sure he'd heard right. He examined the old man's face for hints that a joke was being played on him.

"I'm glad the bloody bastard's dead. Caused me a lifetime of grief, he did. Old man Osbourne Fairfax dealt with Dunham, wouldn't have a thing to do with me. In fact, he almost got me fired as soon as I started here in forty-nine. Never figured what he had his arse in such a knot about, but he did. After he knackered old Dunham to death in sixty-one, he started on me.

"Then, when old man Fairfax died, his son, Sir Reginald took over. He was worse. I couldn't do a bloody thing right. Years of threats and rantings. Gonna turn me in to the coppers or have my licenses pulled, throw me out of the building on my arse, on and on. I tell you, he had a whole bloody bag of threats. Kept me buried with his work, some of it made sense but most of it was pure crap. He didn't want me having other clients. Threatened to take his business away if I took on anybody else."

He was quiet for a moment, taking a private accounting of things. "He did pay ok, though, and I made a living." Just as quickly, he knew his life hadn't really added up to much, "But I learned to hate him."

"Drove me potty. And that 'Sir' thing was a lot of bloody crap, too. He was never knighted, just made it up." Rhetts suddenly stopped, got his breath - a look on his face of exhaustion combined with relief at getting something so vexing off his chest after fifty years. "And I suppose you're going to take up where old Reg left off." The thought of that possibility seemed to wind the old man up for another rant.

"Hey, hold on for a minute," Eddie stopped him, "I don't know what you're talking about. I just showed up . . . uh . . . after I got your email. You said something about an inheritance and reading a will."

Rhetts suddenly looked as if he had lost his train of thought and regarded Eddie through narrowed eyes. "Follow me Fairfax." He pushed himself up from his chair and headed back through the door he had come through minutes before. The second room was bigger but had stacks of books and files on the floor, on tables, in sagging bookcases, all with the same time-worn look of the outer office. An old model push-button phone sat on one corner of another big desk and a computer - so old that Eddie had never seen anything like it - occupied the middle. Can't imagine that thing being able to send an email, Eddie thought.

The old man motioned him to a chair that faced the front of the big desk. "Now look here, Fairfax, you mustn't take me too seriously, you see. I've been angry for fifty years, and just because the last of the Fairfax's is dead doesn't mean I'm ready to forget." Rhetts gave a low chuckle. "But I am happy he's dead. Just wish I'd had something to do with it."

Eddie gave Rhetts the barest of smiles. He didn't want to antagonize the old man just in case he was a real nutter and he certainly didn't want to encourage him in anything rash. "Can we just get on with whatever you're going to do?"

Rhetts gave Eddie a sharp look and began to dig in one of the desk drawers. Eddie stiffened. Was the old coot looking for a gun? Was he going to catch the blame and maybe even a bullet for all those years of whatever Rhetts was stewing about? Eddie wondered just how fast he could dive for the floor when Rhetts pulled a tattered file from the drawer and tossed it on the desk.

"Last thing the old shit said to me before he died," Rhetts said, remembering the insult with bitterness, "was 'you'll probably bugger this up, too, Rhetts.' I thought about doing just that, but then he'd have the satisfaction of being right. Wouldn't think of letting that happen."

Rhetts took a single sheet of paper from the folder, readjusted his glasses and started to read through some legalese. He suddenly stopped and looked up at Eddie. "Hell, Fairfax, it just says you're to inherit an old rundown cottage and a plot of weeds out in a little village a few miles from here – Chipping Campden. Now that you know all about it," he said, moving papers around to indicate the meeting was wrapping up, "I'll get the real paperwork ready in a couple of days. In the meantime, you can go have a look at your grand inheritance." Rhetts gave Eddie a smug smile. "I wouldn't get my hopes up too much, probably just an old pile of stones. If I know old Reginald," Rhetts slammed a veiny hand on one of the stacks, "the old wanker is probably laughing at both of us right now," Rhetts eyes dropped to the floor, "from down there."

Eddie peered at Rhetts through the fine dust he'd kicked up, "I don't quite see how I 'know all about it' as you say."

Rhetts held up a hand to stop Eddie, "Look at the place and we'll go from there. You may want to refuse." Rhetts grunted again to his own amusement.

"Do you know how to find the place?" Eddie asked hopefully.

"Never been there myself. Never invited. Guess it didn't occur to either the old bugger or his worse son to have as guest someone they'd known for half a century. Not good enough, I 'spose. Just as well, too. They gave me enough grief here. Wouldn't go near the place if I had a bloody invite from the queen."

Eddie rephrased the question. "Can you tell me how to find it?"

Rhetts looked at Eddie as if he were suddenly exhausted from their meeting and scribbled on a sheet of paper and handed it across the desk. "Here's the address." Before Eddie could take the paper, Rhetts grabbed it back and scribbled more. "There's my phone number. Call me when you're ready." Rhetts got up and started for the door. Eddie followed and thought about asking 'ready for what?' but his mind was churning with other questions. He needed to get to Chipping Campden.

"Fairfax."

Eddie turned at the sound of his name. Rhetts stood just inside the first office with a look across his wearied features that said he might take a parting shot at the heir of the last Fairfax, a final chance for repayment. "Not the least bit curious?" He asked.

Eddie took his hand from the door knob and turned as he processed the question, "Curious about what?"

"Why you're here, you dumb sod. Never occurred to you once why you'd inherited something from somebody you most likely never heard of?"

Prestonburg had taught Eddie not to respond to every insult thrown his way and it seemed the old man still had something else to get off his chest. Eddie had also learned to listen for the tiniest nugget of useful information that could lie hidden in rants and ramblings.

"Ok, so why Edward . . . uh, me?"

Rhetts gave a slight motion with his head and turned back through the door and took up his place of fifty years behind the desk. Eddie followed and again sat facing him. The big desk, covered in its fine patina of dust, its outdated equipment and useless documents, was as much a barrier in time as it was in space. Rhetts once again searched one of the drawers and seemed lost behind its mass for so long, Eddie was afraid he'd died down there.

Old Rhetts finally reappeared above the desk holding a volume without any identification that Eddie could see. Rhetts shoved papers aside and laid the book down and tapped its cover as he looked at Eddie over his glasses. "Second sons," he said, and began searching its pages for some arcane revelation. "Second sons," he said again, "that mean anything to you?"

Being English, the faintest meaning stirred in the back of Eddie's mind but nothing concrete emerged. "No, "Eddie said.

Rhetts closed the book and started with a story he knew well. "Victorian England operated under a peculiar system for passing on property from one generation to the next. It was called primogeniture, and if you weren't the first born in a family you were bloody well buggered for life. All property was inherited by the first born son and any later born sons were left to fend for themselves, and most of them weren't prepared for that.

"Good ole Thomas Hughes, the Victorian era social reformer and author, thought he had a solution. He managed to set up a colony in America so English second sons would have a place to while away their miserable lives while they dug around in the rock-hard dirt trying to grow enough to keep from starving. Bloody great plan, he had." Rhetts stopped and looked under raised eyebrows at Eddie, "You're following me, Fairfax, right?" He gave a dry chuckle and said, "Apparently not. Let me get on with the rest of it.

"About 1890, Arthur Driscoll Fairfax, himself an unfortunate second son, took up Mr. Hughes offer of a utopian paradise as his best chance of getting on with a decent life and emigrated to America. The family had no contact with him after that time. Meanwhile the family on this side had their good times and their bad and with Sir Reginald, finally came to the end of the miserable line. Sir Reginald must have realized his end was to be soon.

"About two years ago, he had me start checking on Arthur Driscoll Fairfax's branch of the family, see if any of them were still alive." Rhetts laughed cynically, "Wanted to see who he could stick with his bloody 'cottage' just to have one last laugh at their expense. You, Fairfax, are the end of the line on the American side. No wife, no bloody Fairfax offspring." Eddie thought he heard Rhetts mumble something like 'good bloody riddance' under his breath. But you are, apparently, still to be Sir Reginald's heir.

"Well, there you have it. Aren't you the lucky one." Rhetts laughed so hard he began wheezing, stirring up a mini tempest among the papers and dust on his desk. He waved a hand toward the door which Eddie took as a sign that he could leave. He wanted away from this crazy old man and as he reached the door a second time, Rhetts had managed to suppress his coughing fit and yelled after him, "Three days, Fairfax, three days." Eddie pulled the door closed firmly behind himself, hopefully an effective barrier between himself and old Rhetts.

Eddie heard a lock tumble into place as he descended the steps and another as he crossed the lobby. Outside of Prestonburg, he thought, that was the most depressing and uncomfortable place he'd been since his mother's dismal flat in East London when he was a kid. When he got out on the street with the door closed behind him, he turned for one last look at the building where Dunham Solicitors had been reviled and exploited by Edward's forebears for half a century. He started to throw Rhetts' phone number in a trash can, sure he wouldn't be coming back here. Then he remembered it had the address of Edward's cottage in Chipping Campden. He pushed the paper deeper into his pocket. No, he wouldn't be coming back here, that was certain; he expected to find out everything he wanted to know in Chipping Campden.

Eddie stopped for another caffeine hit to clear his thoughts. Was old Rhetts just off his head?   Eddie wondered, or were Edward's ancestors as evil and over-bearing as Rhetts' made them out to be? And what made them that way? Was it some kind of a Fairfax curse? Was he about to find out something he'd rather not know. Whatever it was, Eddie felt like he was closer than he'd ever been to learning something meaningful about Edward.

Good or bad, he felt stronger than ever that whatever he learned would be a breakthrough in his own life. He gulped the last of his coffee and started back to the hotel. He had to tell Vickie about the meeting with Rhetts and get them both to this village of . . . he pulled the piece of paper from his pocket and read the ragged script again . . . Chipping Campden.

As Eddie walked down the corridor of the Redesdale Arms Hotel toward room 310, his thoughts shifted from Claiborne Rhetts to Vickie and what he might find when he opened the door. Would he find her gone, lost on the streets of the town? If she were there, which Vickie would it be? She drove him nuts but at least she was a refreshing change from thinking about his name or now the strange story told by even stranger, old Claiborne Rhetts.

When he inserted the key and pushed open the door, all his senses took a frontal assault. Vickie's clothes were strewn all over the room, rainbow colors draping every surface, the acrid smell of nail polish hanging prickly in the air.

"Whaddya ya think?" A voice emanated from the confused scene. He finally found her among all the litter and would normally respond to the way she was dressed by tearing off his own clothes. Sitting cross-legged on the couch, she was clothed in the smallest pair of knickers he had ever seen and her favorite old T-shirt with holes in all the right places. But what caught his attention were twenty nails, all impossibly different colors. She looked like a day-glow mosaic.

Eddie decided to restrain his natural impulses. "We've got to get out to this village, Chipping Campden." While Vickie waved twenty nails in the air to dry them, he tried best as he could to describe the offices of Dunham Solicitors and what was apparently the last surviving member of the venerable and tortured firm of attorneys, Claiborne Rhetts.

He convinced Vickie to get dressed - and packed – by suggesting that it would soon be time for lunch. In the meantime, he would go down to reception, pay their bill and find out where Chipping Campden was and how to get there. The desk clerk told Eddie there was a bus available from Moreton-in-Marsh to Chipping Campden, but there were several stops and the next bus was not due for over an hour.

Eddie was impatient to get to the village and find Edward's cottage; he decided to hire a cab for the trip. On the drive to Chipping Campden, the English countryside had lost none of its fascination for Vickie as she watched the centuries-old features of the landscape glide by with the attention she'd give to a favorite movie. Eddie chatted with the cabbie who remembered driving someone to Chipping Campden just the afternoon before. The driver offered his opinion that the man sounded like an American.

Was it possible that Edward had somehow found out about his email and beat him there? He didn't think so, but as soon as they got to the village he'd have to get on the internet and check if Edward had found the email in his spam. Eddie asked about hotels but the cabbie regrettably couldn't remember the name of the hotel where he had dropped his previous passenger. He was new to the area, he told Eddie, but then turned with a broad smile, "But don't worry, mate, might not remember the name, but I can take you to it, straightaway."

The cabbie and Eddie soon exhausted things they could talk about and Eddie fell again into thoughts of old Rhetts. Eddie wondered what he'd do without a Fairfax to react to. Maybe he'd just finally fade away, become part of the dust and debris in his old office.

With the quiet and the motion of the car, Eddie dozed off thinking about old Rhetts. The cab soon braked and turned off the A44 and onto the B4081 toward the small village hidden away in the folds of the Cotswold hills. "There she is, mate!" The cabbie sang out and pointed through the windscreen. Eddie sat up and rubbed his eyes. A brilliant sun, undiluted by typical English weather, highlighted spires and angular rooftops. Chipping Campden was still a mile away but seemed to be rising out of its emerald green setting like some golden mirage. Native stone, the color of yellow honey, had been favored for centuries by the builders of scores of Cotswold villages because of its warm, golden glow. Subdued by a long grey winter, the stone now reflected the early summer sun's light. Eddie was mesmerized by an England he'd never seen before and Vickie was now completely in a trance.

The cab descended the long grade into the village and turned right onto the high street. They drove past tiny shop fronts, past a medieval market hall on the left, and straight toward the thin, sky-piercing spire of an ancient church. The cabbie made a quick swerve across traffic and pulled to the curb on the right. "Here we are, mate. That's it," he said, "the Lygon Arms," a note of pride in his voice that he'd been able to find it again.

Eddie and Vickie peered through the windscreen at the small sign identifying the hotel while the cabbie jumped from his seat and began pulling their luggage from the cab's boot. Eddie put his hand on Vickie's arm to keep her in the cab while he looked up and down the village high street for Edward. He was certain he'd recognize him instantly. Edward's face had been in his dreams so often after being seared into his memory in the courtroom. Eddie thought about asking the cabbie what his passenger of the day before had looked like, but sometimes a question like that brought other questions he'd rather not answer.

He motioned for Vickie to get out. He took another look around when he got out but saw no one familiar. Eddie paid the fare, the cab executed a quick u-turn and was quickly on its way out of the village. Like orphans left on a doorstep, they stood a bit bewildered on the sidewalk by the entrance to the hotel. The Lygon Arms had the look of a mini-fortress and was accessed by a high arched doorway cut through the massive stone wall. The entrance was closed off by a great and heavy oak door.

Surrounded by their luggage, they looked at each other and then at the door. The sidewalk and the door itself were a few steps below the level of the high street, a situation that seemed to naturally direct them toward the door. Eddie lifted an iron lever and pushed the door open. The hotel pub, which Vickie quickly spotted, was on the right and ahead was a cobblestone passage separating two sections of the hotel and leading back to another street at the edge of the village. Beyond were tall old trees and rolling pastures. Eddie hadn't thought what they might do if the hotel was full, but luckily there was room available.

They had a late lunch in the pub and at Vickie's request strolled the village for the better part of the afternoon. They poked in every corner and looked in every shop, and Eddie kept a wary eye out for Edward. Eddie laughed as Vickie must have said 'wow' and 'cool' a hundred times as she absorbed the 'strangeness' of The Cotswolds. Finally driven indoors by a late afternoon rainstorm, she gave Eddie her assessment, "I love it. I want to live here."

"Yeah. Right," Eddie laughed.

"No, I mean it," she said. The look on her face was a new one to Eddie. He couldn't imagine her living in a small village.

At dinner, they ate again at the pub and enjoyed several of the local ales. Between the alcohol and residual jetlag, Vickie fell asleep at dusk. Eddie sat by a small lamp and pored over a couple of newspapers to see if there were any stories about Sir Reginald. He found nothing. He was beginning to succumb to travel weariness himself and began to undress. He heard the rattle of paper in his pocket and pulled out the note given him by Rhetts. He looked at the address and softly said in the direction of the sleeping Vickie, "Tomorrow we find Edward's cottage."

Chapter Nine

Chipping Campden, Gloucestershire

"How are we going to get there?" Vickie said between mouthfuls of The Lygon Arms 'full English breakfast.' "I especially like the tomatos and the beans on toast and the ham and eggs."

Eddie laughed, "that's about all of it."

"Yeah, I like it all. How'd you say we're getting there?"

"The lady at the front desk said it was a couple of miles out of the village on the road behind the big church. Said we'd definitely recognize it. I asked her if she had known Sir Reginald."

"Was he really a knight? Isn't that what you said that means?" Vickie asked, spreading jam on slices of granary bread.

"Not according to Rhetts," said Eddie. "And I didn't get much from the front desk about Sir Reginald . . . except a peculiar look."

"You still didn't say how we're getting there?" Vickie said again.

"I guess we'll walk. At a couple of miles it shouldn't take long." Eddie had expected an objection from Vickie when he told her this and was surprised when she smiled and said "cool."

Eddie and Vickie left through the big oak door and turned right toward the thin spire of St. James Church. Eddie surveyed the street for someone who looked like Edward. Even though he'd checked Edward's email and found the message from Claiborne Rhetts still hadn't been opened, the idea that an American had taken a cab to this village just the day before put Eddie on edge. Coincidences had to happen sometimes, he allowed, but he still didn't like it. They walked by the Eight Bells Inn and turned left by the Alms houses. St. James Church lay on a rise to the right. At first sight of the church cemetery's tombstones, Vickie took Eddie's hand and walked close by his side. "Why did the lady at the hotel think we'd recognize the cottage?"

He glanced at her, "It's probably the only total wreck in that neighborhood." He had wondered about that himself, why she had thought he'd recognize it. Probably just something people said. And he'd been careful not to say too much, especially what Rhetts had said about it being a wreck. Still, he was curious, she'd said so confidently that he'd recognize it. It didn't matter, he had the address that Rhetts gave him and he didn't want to stir up too much curiosity with too many questions.

The narrow road that left the village along the back of St. James church descended a gentle hillside between modern houses on the left and a vast open meadow on the right. In the distance they could see the ruins of centuries-old brick structures, the surrounding fields, green as emerald, dotted here and there with fuzzy clumps of grazing sheep.

Both were enjoying the crisp spring morning and the chance to walk off some of the effects of a 'full English breakfast.' Vickie was so taken by the wonder of the countryside that she kept up a chatter as they walked and scanned the area for Edward's cottage.

"Are you going to take his inheritance?" she asked again.

"No, that's not why I came to England," he said a little sharply. "I just thought whatever I could find out about it would help me figure out something important to me, ok? Just leave it alone and stop asking."

"I've read about people like you," Vickie said indifferently.

Eddie gave her a hard look, "What do you mean?"

"You're compulsive. It means you worry about things too much. You've got Edward on the brain."

"I'm compulsive!" He shot back, "you're the one who keeps talking about taking his inheritance."

The very idea had a despicable sound to it. Stealing a little of somebody's money was one thing, but an inheritance was different. How it was different, he wasn't quite sure. He just wished Vickie would leave it alone.

They walked on in silence, both looking for something that fit either the description of 'cottage' or 'total wreck.'

At a crossroads, a sign indicated that Chipping Campden was four miles behind them. "We missed it somehow," Eddie said. They turned back toward the village determined to be more attentive to anything that looked like a cottage. When the first houses of the village began appearing again on the right and the familiar ruins off to the left, they stopped again and looked at each other, mystified.

"What does a cottage look like anyway?" Vickie asked. "The only thing half-way along was that drive that went over the big hill. Just disappeared out of sight, but I didn't see anything."

Eddie thought about her question, but since his childhood home in London had been a world of tenements, not cottages, he didn't really know. "That has to be it," he said. "Let's go back and ask. If the drive's not to the cottage, it could be to a neighbor's place and they might be able to help us."

Minutes later Vickie and Eddie were at the lone drive cutting off the main road. They looked to where the road, little more than a track, climbed the long hill and disappeared over the top. They began walking along the hard packed dirt lane hidden between parallel rows of tall poplar trees. Soon a small building appeared at a gentle turn in the track. It hadn't been visible from the main road, hidden behind stands of large trees. Another minute of brisk walking and they were standing at the door to the cottage. Both were breathing heavily.

"Let's stop for a minute," Vickie said, "I need a rest. I'm not used to climbing hills."

"I think this is it," he said. "Go and rest on that bench while I knock." He pointed at a thick slab of stone laid across two upright stones. "Maybe someone's here that can tell us if we're at the right place."

Several series of vigorous knocks on the door brought no response. Eddie peered through the dusty windows on either side of the door but saw no signs that anyone had recently lived there.

"There's not even any furniture," he said over his shoulder to Vickie. "Maybe after the old man died they emptied the place out."

He walked to where Vickie rested on the stone bench and sat beside her. Eddie welcomed the rest, too. They looked around them as they caught their breath and saw that now the drive itself was not just lined with rows of trees but surrounded on both sides by dense forest.

Unable to see further than a few feet left or right, Eddie stood on the stone block and peered down the drive where the trees seemed to pull away from the road on both sides. "There's some kind of big building ahead. I can just see its roofline. Let's ask there. Maybe they'll know where the cottage is if this isn't it.

Eddie reached for Vickie's hand and helped her to her feet. "You still like England?" he laughed as she reluctantly got to her feet. They started along the drive toward the distant roofline.

"Yeah, I love it," she said, now breathing easier.

Eddie was surprised and pleased at seeing a new side of Vickie. She was excited by something besides eating, sleeping and nail polish.

Ten minutes later the building began to take on a distinct shape as the drive widened and the trees receded on either side. "Wow," Vickie said. That building's huge."

They stopped and surveyed the house and its grounds. Neither Eddie nor Vickie had the slightest experience with anything similar to the building that seemed to occupy the entire horizon. It was like asking someone from their apartment building on 177th street to estimate the size and worth of a luxury high rise tower on Park Ave. "This place looks like money – old money – people that've been around here for a long, long time," Eddie said. "Probably knows of everything and everyone within miles. I'm betting they'll know of old Reginald and where he lived. Let's go." They picked up their pace and started for the distant building.

Eddie thought it was strange that with a house this big there were no cars visible. The fine gravel drive that had replaced the packed earth road they had just climbed across the hill was full of tire marks.

Eddie hoped that meant someone was there to help them. They couldn't climb every hill in the area looking for Edward's cottage. They were city people and unaccustomed to slogging across steep hills.

Eddie crossed his fingers and lifted the massive iron knocker mounted in the center of the great double oaken doors. The result of dropping the iron weight sounded like a huge gong outside; he could only imagine what it sounded like inside. While they waited, Eddie and Vickie turned back to look at the broad drive they had just walked.

The effect was like looking into a funnel as the trees swept in from both right and left with the road seeming to disappear down the funnel's dark throat. Eddie had a strange feeling that made no sense. He looked at Vickie who was already staring up at him with an uneasy look on her face. A creaking sound made them both jump. The door swung open. A broad-chested, heavy-set man in liveried attire stood ramrod straight, his stiff form filling most of the door opening. His age was indeterminate, but probably much older than someone in personal service should be, Eddie thought.

His size and stiff demeanor were a bit intimidating but a faint hint of a smile he wore on a scrubbed looking face let Eddie and Vickie relax enough to ask their question. "Hello," said Eddie, "hoping you could help with some directions."

" Certainly, sir, how can I be of help?"

"We're looking for a small cottage owned by a Reginald Fairfax."

The big man's smile broadened, "Well, sir, it seems you've found it on first go."

Both Eddie and Vickie turned around to search the neighboring landscape, surprised that they had somehow walked right by it without noticing. Nothing but deep woods. Eddie had expected this search might not be easy, but it was getting more difficult than he had imagined. He had no desire to go tramping through those woods looking for some pile of stones as old Rhetts had described it. And if he was supposed to be able to recognize it, why was it so hard to find?

Eddie turned back to face the man, "It wouldn't be the place we passed on the track up the hill, would it?"

"No sir, as I said, you've found it," the man replied. "This is it."

Eddie and Vickie looked at each other, bewildered. Eddie was also feeling a bit frustrated. The man's accent sounded virtually the same as his but apparently he wasn't communicating.

"We're looking for a small cottage, probably a ruin, maybe even deserted now. It was owned by a Reginald Fairfax. He's just recently passed away. Do you know of him or where he lived?" That was as plain as he knew how to put it, Eddie thought and he watched the man's eyes for a sense of comprehension. Quit smiling, dammit, Eddie was thinking, and just answer my question. The smile left the big man's face as he turned and nodded toward the building behind him.

"As I said, this is Sir Reginald's 'cottage' as you so curiously refer to it," the man said dryly. "And I assume you would be Mr. Edward Fairfax."

Eddie took a couple of steps backward trying to make sense of what the man had just said. He knew his name. Even worse, since he had used Edward's name, Edward must be expected – any minute. He looked back at Vickie who shrugged her shoulders and pulled a face. "But the solicitor, Mr. Rhetts, said it was just probably a pile of stones," was the only way Eddie could respond. The old man was making no sense.

He took a couple of more steps back and looked up at the massive façade of the huge building. It was four stories high, had dozens of windows across the wide expanse and massive towers on either end. To Eddie, It looked like a whole block in New York. He'd managed to get Vickie across the Atlantic, through customs, through London, and finally to the right village in far west England and now it seemed he had come to a dead end. This was crazy.

"I assume that you would be Mr. Edward Fairfax," the man said again.

Eddie looked back at the man and nodded. . .and swallowed hard.

"I'm Chalmers," the man said

Eddie watched the man's eyes. Then he looked at Vickie who hadn't yet realized they might be in danger.

Somehow this man already knew they were looking for Sir Reginald's cottage. Had Rhetts already decided that he and Vickie were imposters and alerted the countryside to be on the lookout for them? Eddie wondered if he could simply apologize for the interruption, thank this man for his time and quickly head back into the mouth of the forest funnel and get away from here.

"Then you would be Mister Edward Fairfax," the man said again.

Eddie closed his mouth and looked in the man's eyes again. He saw no hint of trickery or danger. What was he thinking, of course, they'd be expecting Edward. This man would be a neighbor of Sir Reginald, he would be aware that Sir Reginald had died, and in the way of small communities know something of everybody else's business. He'd know that Sir Reginald was expecting his heir. At least, the dilapidated cottage was expecting its heir. Calm down, he told himself. He took a deep breath and told a lie, "Yes, I am. I'm Edward Fairfax."

Vickie grabbed Eddie's hand, squeezed it hard and hissed in his ear, "Eddie, you're being weird again. Just stop it! This man is trying to tell you that this is Sir Reginald's house."

Chalmers turned his gaze on Vickie. His eyes subtly took in the red hair, the unavoidable spectacle of nails, but gave no hint of surprise or disapproval. He evenly asked, "And you, miss, would be?"

"I'm Mrs. Fairfax . . .Vickie." She was smiling broadly at Chalmers, apparently now getting comfortable with her new name.

Chalmers gave a small bow and stepped back in to the doorway. "Please, do come in. We've been expecting you."

Eddie looked at Vickie and saw no hesitation on her part. Expected or not, Eddie was uncomfortable with the fact that Chalmers already knew his name. He half expected to walk inside and find old Rhetts sitting behind a dust-covered desk with a large shotgun aimed at them.

Worried or not, he felt an irresistable hand pushing him through the door. His thoughts raced back to the time four years before when his initial curiosity about Edward had been his downfall. Had he let it happen again? Had he given in to an obsession and walked into the same trap again. Maybe even Edward was there to enjoy and mastermind his second downfall. That was the American the cabbie had brought to Chipping Campden yesterday. He was here, that's why Eddie hadn't seen him in the village. Suddenly, Eddie felt sick. Chalmers had said 'we' were expecting you. Then, what else could that mean? Could he possibly think Eddie had anything to do with Reginald's death?

With Eddie and Vickie both inside, Chalmers reached up beside the massive door and gave a pull on a gold colored tassel, its attached cord disappearing into the wall. The cavernous room was slowly coming into focus in the dim light. Eddie tried to take it in without being too obvious. The room was enormous. Walls rose to unlikely heights and the expanse of marble floor seemed to glide unchecked into distant shadows.

A huge chandelier with its dozens of bulbs that would have set most reasonably-sized rooms ablaze with its light did little more than offer a feeble challenge to the darkness in this grand entry. Far away, a broad staircase rose from the center of the immense space, dividing and turning in both directions, continuing to climb. As his eyes continued to adjust and he could take in more features around him, Eddie was becoming more and more uneasy and saw that Chalmers was watching his reaction. He thought about how many corners in this place there were for old Rhetts to be hiding in the dark ready to spring out and . . .

"Sir, I beg your pardon," he heard Chalmers saying, "I fear I've left you hanging a bit and haven't quite answered your question." Eddie was suddenly trying to remember what his question had been. Yes, he now remembered - where was old Reginald's cottage? Eddie turned back toward Chalmers who was tugging at the tasseled cord again. Vickie was engrossed and staring at the ceiling.

"The building you passed on the way up the track was the old gatehouse of the manor. We don't use it anymore since Sir Reginald's father built a new entrance on the other side of the house. This," Chalmers swung his arm around the room, "is Sir Reginald's cottage, as you so quaintly call it."

Eddie's chin dropped. Before he could process - much less answer - this shocking statement, he heard footfalls approaching in the distant gloom. Old Rhetts really was there, but for what purpose. The old man was crazy without question and crazy people needed no rational reasons for their actions. Eddie looked back to Chalmers for some clue, perhaps a look that said he should break for the door or simply surrender on whatever favorable terms he could beg. Vickie, he fearfully realized, was to be of no help. She was entirely taken in by it all, mesmerized and neutralized.

He faced Chalmers again, waiting for whatever he and old Rhetts had planned. Eddie expected and could almost feel a cold, bony hand clamp down to grip his shoulder, leaving him powerless and unable to move, denying his escape. On the one side he could hear Chalmers saying his name and on the other he heard the footfalls coming closer, at any moment to reveal their form from the shadows. After that experience at Prestonburg, he berated himself, how had he been trapped again? He swallowed hard and felt a tremble take control of his hands. He suddenly felt the hand settle on his shoulder. He waited for the paralyzing pressure. The hand ready to disable his movements, the approaching footsteps, the voice calling his name, his own hands trembling. Now another hand, another voice calling, "Eddie, what's wrong with you?"

Eddie shook his head to clear away the memory. It was Vickie with her hand on his shoulder. "Eddie, what's wrong? Are you ok?" He nodded and looked toward Chalmers.

"Are you well, sir?" Chalmers now wore a look of concern. Eddie knew he was overreacting. "Yeah, I'm ok. Just a bit tired I guess."

Chalmers motioned to the source of the footfalls behind Eddie. "Sir, this is my granddaughter, Evie. She will prepare some refreshments for you and Mrs. Fairfax. Please follow me to the parlor where you can rest. I will be quite pleased to answer all your questions."

Evie gave them a slight nod, "Sir, maam." She turned back in the direction she had come and Chalmers led them to a high door at the rear of the reception hall. The parlor was totally different from the entry. It had tall, broad windows allowing the early afternoon sun to warm the room and show off the exquisite antiques that lent the whole room an aspect of comfort and friendliness – and old wealth. Eddie started to relax. Vickie was taking everything in as if making an inventory.

"Sir, may I inquire as to where you and Mrs. Fairfax are lodging?"

"Uh . . . we're at the Lygon Arms," Eddie said hesitantly.

"Oh my, you're already staying in the village. We can't have you staying elsewhere when you are going to be the next proprietor, now can we?"

"Thank you Chalmers, but we couldn't . . . I mean we can't . . . "

"Oh Eddie, can we?" squealed Vickie. "Please, I'd love to stay. As Mr. Chalmers said, you . . . uh, . . we are going to be the next . . ."

Eddie gave Vickie a warning look but to no effect. She answered Chalmers directly. "Yeah, we'll stay but our bags are at the hotel."

"Not a problem, Maam. I'll send Nigel down to the village with the estate car and retrieve them."

Who was this person, Eddie was beginning to wonder, when he saw that Vickie was planning to settle in.

They needed to talk, Eddie thought. This wasn't like her. Well, on second thought, it was very much like her, he decided. She'd settled in with a total stranger when he had rented the apartment and now this would be her idea of trading up.

"If it's agreeable to you, Sir, and to Mrs. Fairfax," Chalmers interrupted his thoughts, "let me show you to your rooms now and we can talk tonight after you've rested. We'll serve dinner at half past seven in the dining hall and I will be most happy to answer your queries in the Hunt Room afterwards. It does get a bit chilly in this big old pile of stone in the evening this time of year. I'll see that a nice fire is laid in the hearth. Makes conversation much more agreeable."

Good, Eddie thought. A chance to sort things out with Vickie. "Yes, Chalmers, that's nice of you. We can talk after dinner."

"Come with me then, Sir." Chalmers led them out of the parlor and started up the broad central staircase. At the second landing he turned down a wide corridor lit by small but exquisite sconces, each one casting a halo of yellow light only far enough to touch the next halo – giving a scalloped effect but no idea how far the corridor extended. Underfoot was deep pile carpeting that swallowed the sound of their footsteps as they followed Chalmers. He stopped in front of a large double set of doors recessed in the wall and produced a key from his vest pocket. He turned it in the lock and pushed one of the doors open.

Eddie immediately saw that they were on the other side of the house from the parlor. No sun streamed in through the tall windows. A quick look at the ancient poplar trees outside the windows showed their shadows falling just behind them. Eddie had lost track of time but without looking at his watch he knew it was already early afternoon from the shadows.

"I'll leave you to rest and when Nigel returns with your bags I'll have him bring them up." Chalmers turned back toward the door.

"Thank you, Chalmers," Vickie cooed.

Eddie closed the door as quietly as he could and threw the lock. He turned to see Vickie inspecting the huge bed, complete with brocaded canopy and counterpane. "Wow," she said, rubbing her hands across the heavy fabrics. "This place is unbelievable!" She turned her back to the bed and jumped up and landed on the edge, bouncing. "Can you believe all that stuff downstairs in that room he called the parlor? There must be a fortune in stuff down there. And look at this bedroom. It looks more like a king or queen should be sleeping here instead of us. But do you know the best part?"

Eddie walked to the bed and put both hands on her shoulders to stop the bouncing, "No, I don't see a good part to this right now. Why does Chalmers want us here? What was wrong with us staying in the village and why did you say what you did? Why did you say we'd like to stay here without even talking to me? I think that crazy old Rhetts is hanging about here, too. I don't trust him."

"I wouldn't trust him either. He must be crazy calling this place a cottage. Stop worrying." Vickie said with a surprising ring of authority in her voice. "Why shouldn't we stay here? After all, it's going to belong to us soon."

Eddie backed up. He couldn't believe what he'd just heard. "Are you nuts? This is Edward's. I just wanted to come see the place, that's all. It could help me understand him and how he got past . . .

"Why?" Vickie shouted. She wore a look that both surprised him and backed him into a mental corner.

Why *did* he want to see the place, he asked himself, his mind racing to find an answer that he could give her. Her different look and attitude were making him uncomfortable. He'd never made himself answer his own questions before and now this new Vickie had suddenly demanded something more of him. Now he was at a place where he could not simply brush her off because . . . now . . . he wanted that question answered, too.

"Let's wait until tonight when we talk to Chalmers," Eddie said. "Obviously, old Chalmers doesn't know Edward but knows a lot about him, which means," he said as directly to Vickie as he could with her continuing appraisal of the room and its furnishings, "we have to be careful and not say anything that's different from what he knows."

"So how do we know what he knows?" Vickie snapped back.

"We don't. We just listen and don't talk. That way we learn what he knows and he doesn't find out what we don't know."

Vickie thought about the logic of Eddie's argument for a few seconds, "Ok, but I really like this place. . .and I like England. You're not thinking of giving up your inheritance, are you?"

For the second time in minutes he was astonished by this new Vickie. "I told you, this is Edward's inheritance, not mine."

"But you steal his money. What's the difference between that and taking his inheritance? Just a lot more of it," she said.

"It's not funny," he shot back. "Just wait 'til tonight and give me a chance to think this through." Eddie was trying to decide what the difference between taking Edward's money and his inheritance really was, if in fact there was any difference at all.

"Come here," Vickie reached out and took his hand and pulled Eddie toward her as she lay back on the plump bed.

"Nigel will be here with our bags soon," Eddie protested weakly.

"He'll knock," Vickie said as she playfully gripped his earlobe between her teeth.

Chapter Ten

Fairfax Manor - Chipping Campden.

Eddie and Vickie were awakened by a sharp knocking at the door. Eddie sat up in the bed and for a moment was unable to remember where he was. He looked around the strange room with its old-fashioned furniture and heavily draped windows trying to make sense of things.

"What are you doing?"

He turned to face the voice and got a sharp poke in the ribs, "That's probably our bags," Vickie hissed, "that man was going to bring them from the hotel."

Eddie slid from the big bed and tiptoed to the door. He found their bags waiting just outside in the corridor;

Nigel was already out of sight. Whoever Nigel was, Eddie thought, he was efficient and stealthy. They had slept away most of the afternoon in the huge, luxurious bed. Eddie brought everything into the room, laid his bag on the floor and quickly put on some fresh clothes. Vickie seemed determined to achieve just the right look and changed into her third, then fourth outfit. Eddie waited impatiently and looked around the room. He pulled back the draperies and saw that a broad cobblestone drive swept away from the house and divided a well kept lawn accented here and there with various shrubbery, some cut into shapes resembling different animals.

He realized that the windows looked out toward the front of the house and that he and Vickie had apparently approached the house from the back. That made sense, he thought. A house like this wouldn't have a packed dirt track as its main entry way. By the time Vickie had decided on her look for dinner and they arrived down stairs, it was well past seven.

Evie was waiting in the grand entry to show them to the dining hall. It was an enormous high-ceilinged room dominated by a long ornate wooden table surrounded by at least thirty chairs. Gilded frames held the portraits of several Fairfax ancestors who seemed to stare accusingly down at Eddie.

He had to stop Vickie from inventorying the room when he realized that Evie was taking notice of their reactions to everything. They sat facing each other at one end of the table and waited until Evie left the room before Eddie leaned closer. "Would you stop doing that?"

"What?" Vickie said sharply.

"Drooling over everything" Eddie said and nodded his head at the departing girl. "She was watching you. They'll think we're going to steal the candle sticks."

"Why would we steal what's gonna be ours?" Vickie snapped back, "and besides, I don't like her."

"Why would you say that? You don't even know her," he asked exasperated and surprised. "And I'd already asked you to wait until. . ." Eddie stopped as Evie reappeared carrying a large pot. She placed it directly between them and the aroma of roasted meat instantly washed over their senses. Both remembered that their last meal had been hours ago. Evie produced a large silver ladle and began to serve what she said was one of Sir Reginald's favorite dishes, a slow-cooked, rich meat soup made from game caught on the estate.

"Isn't Chalmers going to eat with us?" Eddie asked.

"Oh no sir. The staff doesn't eat in this dining room. We have a dining room near the kitchen. Although," she said thoughtfully, "my grandfather did dine occasionally with Sir Reginald. That's very unusual, you know, for any staff to dine with the master of the house." There was a note of pride in Evie's voice. "But Sir Reginald was like that," she added. Eddie caught a wistful look as if a warm and favorite memory had just ghosted through her thoughts.

They ate quietly as Evie brought other courses, Vickie's attention riveted on the food instead of the room and its furnishings. Finally, with the last one Eddie looked with amusement at Vickie over the flickering candle, "If you like everything about England, you're going to love this," he waved his spoon at the dessert that Evie had just brought. "It's called sticky toffee pudding."

"That's a weird name," Vickie said as she cautiously took a bite. Her look said she half expected that Eddie might be tricking her into eating something disgusting for his own entertainment. She cautiously took a nibble and soon a soft "uummm" floated across the table and Eddie watched the sticky toffee pudding disappear as Vickie's spoon flashed in the candlelight like a sabre in a duel. She wore a supremely satisfied look when Evie returned with the news that Chalmers waited in the Hunt Room. Evie led them back across the main entry hall to a room they hadn't yet seen.

As they walked through the dimness of the great reception hall, a yellow light flickered through a half opened door as they approached. Eddie could already smell the pleasant aroma of the wood smoke.

Evie left them at the door. Chalmers was standing at the hearth, pushing a large log around on the grate. Sparks flew and the fire brightened. Nervous shadows danced about the room. Chalmers turned and waved them to chairs facing the fire. "Sir, maam, I trust you had a pleasant dinner."

"Wow, yes, I loved that softee pudding dessert thing," Vickie said.

Chalmers chuckled as he put the fire tool back in its place and took a chair facing them. "It's one of my favorites, as well, Mrs. Fairfax." He settled into the sturdy wingback chair and crossed his legs. "Evie will have coffee and brandy for us in a few moments, Sir. In the meanwhile, let me see if I can answer some questions for you."

Oh, if only you could, thought Eddie. Fortunately, Vickie was doing another of her inventories of the rich furnishings of the room and wasn't answering Chalmer's herself.

"Yeah," Eddie said. He tried to get comfortable in his big wingback and wished that he could ask Chalmers what he knew about Edward. "Can you tell me something about Sir Reginald? Rhetts says he was quite a rough man. . .with him, at least."

Chalmers smiled, his teeth flashing in the firelight. "Sir Reginald was a fine gentlemen, highly esteemed by all who knew and dealt with him. Certainly, by me and all the staff here at Fairfax Hall. He was most generous, I would say, and all the neighbors here about would agree that he was a fair and reasonable man." Chalmers interrupted his glowing eulogy as Evie pushed in a cart with tinkling cups and pots and began pouring coffee.

"But old Rhetts," Eddie said a bit confused by the difference in their stories, "said Sir Reginald gave him a bad time. And had done so for years." he added.

Chalmers accepted the cup offered him by Evie and took a slow sip. A look passed between them that Eddie couldn't interpret.

"You'll have to understand, Sir, that Rhetts is an odd one," Chalmers said, "always has been." Eddie thought he saw Evie nod her agreement in the shadows. She handed Vickie and Eddie their cups and was gone from the room.

"Back when Sir Reginald was a boy of perhaps ten or twelve years old," Chalmers began, "his mother took up with Solicitor Dunham and deserted the boy and his father here at Fairfax Hall. She eventually married Dunham. Master Ambrose Fairfax, Sir Reginald's father was quite devastated, as much for the boy's sake as for himself. But he wasn't a man to accept such disgrace lightly. He waited on his revenge patiently and his opportunity eventually came.

" In some important business matter – I don't quite remember the facts - Dunham made a rather grievous error in judgment and eventually lost everything he owned. And of course, in time the former Mrs. Fairfax - Sir Reginald' mother - finally realized the scope of her mistake and left Dunham just as she had Fairfax. But to Fairfax's way of thinking that didn't let Dunham off the hook.

"Fairfax then brilliantly contracted Dunham's firm to handle some of his legal matters. Nothing important, mind you, but it was a salvation for Dunham who apparently was in such a pickle that he never thought to ask himself why a man whose wife he had stolen might want to help him out of a bind. Unfortunately, for him, he didn't suspect that he had merely struck a deal with the devil. Fairfax tied Dunham up tight as an old lady's corset and then badgered him mercilessly and eventually drove old Dunham over the edge; hung himself.

"Rhett's only mistake was having joined up with the Dunham firm. With Dunham finally off the hook, so to speak, Rhetts was the new whipping boy and totally dependent on Fairfax business. And if Ambrose Fairfax had been bitter over the loss of his wife, then Sir Reginald was doubly determined that someone should pay for the loss of his mother." Chalmers stopped his story for another sip from his cup. "And of course," he continued, "Rhetts was the only target to shoot at. Quite unfortunate, really, Rhetts had nothing to do with any of it, save his being a convenient target."

Chalmers took another sip of his coffee and said, "Can't say that I agree with what Sir Reginald and his father have done but I do believe I can understand why. That's a mighty blow for a man to take, losing his wife to another man. And of course, the boy with no mother. It wasn't easy."

Eddie could understand that. He had lost a father. And no, it wasn't easy. He was intrigued by Chalmer's story. "Why didn't old Rhetts just walk away?" Eddie wanted to know.

"Oh, he tried," said Chalmers, "he tried. But he'd gotten himself so bound up in the affairs of Dunham that he couldn't free himself. And of course, there was his odd personality. It was as if he wanted to stay and fight. It became as much his battle as it had been Dunham's. And for Sir Reginald, Rhetts continued to give him an outlet for his anger. I think Rhetts was somehow disappointed when Sir Reginald finally . . ."

Chalmers cleared his throat and quickly took a long draw from his cup. He gave Eddie the impression that he was afraid he'd already said too much. And Eddie wasn't convinced that Rhetts was that disappointed.

"Sir Reginald never trusted a woman enough to marry and knew he'd never have an heir. Rhetts had to pay for that too. A couple of years ago, Sir Reginald decided to give Rhetts the task of finding out if any relatives might still be alive and living in America. Relatives of a second son." Eddie listened as Chalmers told the strange story of primogeniture and of second sons that he'd already heard from old Rhetts.

"It sounds as if you really liked Sir Reginald," said Eddie.

"Oh, quite right, Sir. We were actually good friends."

"Rhetts said the 'Sir' thing was a lot of bull." Eddie wanted to test his story.

Chalmers smiled again. "Rhetts is quite wrong. Sir Reginald was given the honor by Her Majesty personally. After the war, Sir Reginald distinguished himself in MI6. He helped uncover The Cambridge Five, that Kim Philby and his Ruskie loving traitors. The Queen knighted Sir Reginald for that."

Eddie was impressed but knew that Fairfax Hall couldn't be the result of heroic work in MI6 no matter how much he'd pleased the queen. Apparently, Vickie had finished appraising the room and was listening. The same question was on her mind. "So where did all the money come from," she asked.

Chalmers, far from thinking her impertinent, answered, "That's an excellent question, Mrs. Fairfax. No, one doesn't get rich working for Her Majesty's government. Sir Reginald's wealth goes back several generations. His great-grandfather, Alfred Fairfax, fought in the Boer War in South Africa. He met and formed a close friendship with a young mining pioneer by the name of Cecil Rhodes. When Rhodes founded De Beers Diamond Mines, Mr. Fairfax was eventually made a minor partner. That was the foundation of his wealth. He was an excellent businessman and turned that lucky break into a very large fortune."

Eddie figured that Vickie's next question was 'just how big is the fortune' so when Chalmers reached for the fire tool to stir up the logs again, Eddie took her hand and shook his head; no more questions.

"Er, . . .uh. . .when did Sir Reginald . . .uh. . . .pass on?" Eddie asked.

"It was quite recently, really," Chalmers said as he continued to move the logs around on the grate.

'Quite recently' was a strange way to answer his question, Eddie thought. And would 'natural death' be the correct way to explain Sir Reginald's departure? Eddie wondered. After hearing Chalmers' story and seeing how strange old Rhetts was, Eddie's mind was beginning to imagine several different scenarios, all of which gave him a feeling of uneasiness.

"Since the estate is quite self-sustaining," Chalmers continued, "Sir Reginald made arrangements for all the staff to remain with the estate until the heir was in place." Chalmers replaced the poker on its hook and stood with his back to the fire. The friendly and expressive face now hidden in shadow, gave no clue to the meaning of the next statement, "I'm afraid that Sir Reginald won't fully rest in peace until his heir is in place here at Fairfax Hall.

"Well, Sir," Chalmers rubbed his hands together, "I won't go on with my ramblings. I'm quite sure you and Mrs. Fairfax must be tired after a long and unusual day. I hope you rest well and we shall talk further in the morning." Chalmers excused himself and left Eddie and Vickie alone with the yellow flickers of the fire dancing between the shadows. The huge room with dark corners only occasionally illuminated by the dancing firelight make Eddie very uneasy. He motioned for Vickie to follow him out of the room, across the reception hall and up the broad staircase. Just as they were approaching their room, Eddie thought he heard a lock quietly slide into place in the adjoining door.

Back in their room, Eddie secured the door with the heavy dead bolt. Vickie climbed back on the bed and was about to explode with excitement. "Can you believe all that? Did you see all the stuff in that room? It looks like a museum. I can't believe that just two months ago I was getting evicted from my apartment and now we're going to inherit this huge place and a fortune." She started to bounce giddily on the bed. Eddie walked over to try calming her but simply climbed up on the big bed beside her.

His mind was reeling with what he'd heard from Chalmers and he hadn't nearly enough time to process what it meant. He thought about her question. What was the difference between stealing Edward's money and stealing his inheritance? Really, was there a difference?

"Eddie," he heard her saying as she had picked up one of his hands and squeezed it between hers, "Didn't you say all we had to do was to let that old man Rhetts know when we were ready and then you would inherit all this and then we could move in here and then we wouldn't have to go back to New York and we'd have all this money and. . ."

"Quiet," he told her, "calm down and take a breath." He had to admit it sounded easy. He was beginning to feel the sense of excitement that gripped Vickie. He now had to think about the options he had. He could continue making his living out of ATM machines and always be looking over his shoulder or he could become an estate owner and live off a huge inheritance, never having to worry from day to day, not looking over his shoulder.

That wasn't a difficult choice he told himself. But could they pull it off? What would he do about Edward if and when he learned about Fairfax Manor? He sure wasn't going to roll over and say it was ok to nick his inheritance. He even told himself he'd miss the excitement of his present life and he did enjoy his creative work with the computer.

Then he remembered that it had been a couple of days since he had checked Edward's email. With what he now knew, he realized he couldn't let Edward read what was hidden away in his spam folder. He needed more time to sort out all this information and as far as he knew, there was no internet connection at Fairfax Hall. In fact, he hadn't seen any evidence that it had even entered the telephone age. "We'll ask Chalmers to take us into town tomorrow."

Chapter Eleven

Fairfax Manor - Chipping Campden

While Vickie enjoyed another marathon shower, Eddie went down to the dining hall with the hope of finding a cup of coffee. Evie had set the same two places at the end of the grand table with breakfast fare. As Eddie poured coffee from the thermos, he heard the approach of footfalls and turned to see the proper face of Chalmers. "Good morning, Sir. I trust you were comfortable, and Mrs. Fairfax as well."

"Yeah, thanks." Eddie smiled. "Could we get a lift into town this morning?"

"Certainly, Sir. May I make any arrangements for you before you go?"

"Certainly, Chalmers, that's quite good of you to ask." Eddie smiled when he heard his own answer. He was quickly getting the hang of being a potential manor house owner. The idea of having someone to take care of tiresome little chores was an appealing thought, something he could get used to. And Vickie could be very persuasive.

She was probably right, there was no difference in taking a guy's money from his bank account and taking his inheritance. It was just a matter of scale, he told himself, and the size of Edward's debt to him was pretty big.

"I think we would like to see Rhetts today and finish up whatever paperwork that's required." Eddie's smile grew even wider thinking of the enormous benefits of putting his name on a few documents. "Perhaps you could ring Rhetts and tell him we'll be in right after breakfast."

"Most certainly, Sir, but I'm afraid Nigel has the estate car off to Cheltenham on an errand. He should be back by early afternoon. But I'll ring Rhetts and ask him to be prepared. Perhaps 2:00 in the afternoon. Is there anything else, Sir?"

Eddie wanted to access Edward's email a lot sooner but decided he wouldn't push Chalmers.

"Ah. . . .no, I don't think so." Eddie wondered what sort of things Sir Reginald would have answered to 'is there anything else?' and decided that since he was new to this master of the house role, Chalmers wouldn't expect anything.

He'd work on that after his visit to Rhett's office today.

Eddie turned to go back up to their room but stopped after a couple of steps. There was something else Chalmers could do, "We'd like to have breakfast in our room today."

"Certainly, Sir. I'll have Evie bring it up straight-away." Chalmers turned on his heel and went off to the kitchen. Eddie thought he saw a sour smile form on Chalmers' lips just as he turned.

So this is what being rich feels like, Eddie thought to himself. Just ask for it and it's yours. While he climbed the broad staircase to their room, he thought about the other possible perks of being rich and realized this was what he wanted.

He hadn't thought about his name in two days. If that was a benefit of being rich, then he knew he had made the right decision. That thought surprised him. He had actually arrived at a decision without realizing it. And then Eddie remembered that Edward owed him something special. Edward had incurred a very large debt. How large? Eddie couldn't say for sure because it was hard to put a price tag on four years of a man's life. What a beautiful way to settle Edward's debt, Eddie thought. And it was a legitimate debt.

Vickie was right, he told himself again, now thor-oughly convinced, there really was no difference be-tween taking a man's money from an ATM and taking his inheritance, especially, if he had never expected the inheritance. Eddie was smiling, and if the man didn't even know about it, how could he ever miss it? He could see now how smart it had been to bring Vickie along. She had a way of seeing simple solutions. And some-times simple was best. He had let himself get lost in the forest and couldn't see the trees. He had been so obsessed with getting Edward's help in dealing with the problems caused by his name that he hadn't realized that Edward had already provided him the answer – being rich solved a lot of problems.

Now, all he had to do was to reach out and grasp it. He opened the door to find Vickie sitting cross-legged on the bed waving her nails in the air. "I changed the colors," she said.

In spite of the acrid bite of nail polish solvent in the air, he generously promised, "You can change color every day after we see old Rhetts today. And," he held out his chest, "I've asked Chalmers to serve breakfast in our room."

Vickie grinned, "I've never done that before."

"But you could get used to it," Eddie said as a soft rap at the door announced Evie and breakfast.

Vickie and Eddie sat in silence, enjoying their own thoughts as they finished off another big breakfast. The gnawing, empty feeling in their stomachs of a few days before was now gone. This was definitely better.

Afterwards, Evie came back to retrieve the cart and confirmed that her grandfather had arranged the meeting with Rhetts. Nigel would be available to take them to the village at half-past one.

Eddie warned Vickie about the state of Rhett's office. He was shocked again at the decrepit mess but figured that after this visit, he would never have to come to this place again. In fact, he would probably put the old man out of his misery and fire him when he became the master of Fairfax Manor.

They stood expectantly in front of the door to the office of Dunham Solicitors and Eddie dropped the heavy knocker. Vickie jumped at the gong like sound. Only seconds passed before Rhetts swung open the door and wordlessly motioned for them to follow him to the second office. Eddie watched Vickie's reaction. It was probably the same as his had been if he could have watched himself.

Nothing had changed except that the chair had a lighter coating of dust on the seat where old Rhetts had used his handkerchief to clean it. Eddie quickly followed Rhetts movement toward the second office and saw that he was wearing the same ancient shiny-seated pants. There were two chairs already placed in front of Rhetts' desk. "This probably won't take long at all," Eddie quietly whispered to Vickie.

They took the two seats and waited while Rhetts dropped into his seat and began digging in one of the side drawers of the desk. He pulled a thin file and carefully placed it on the desk and sat staring at them, from one to the other. The old man sure had a way of making him feel uncomfortable. Eddie noticed that the stacks of files and documents practically covering the desk top at his first visit had been removed. Now the dust shadows were all that remained.

Rhetts still had said nothing but flipped open the folder. It contained only one sheet of paper. Eddie was encouraged. This was going to be even easier than he had thought. Rhetts lifted a corner and turned the sheet around until it faced Eddie and Vickie. The light in the office was too dim to read it from where they sat so they waited to see if Rhetts had flipped the paper as an invitation to read it themselves or if he would read it to them.

Rhetts cleared his throat and tapped the sheet of paper with a bony finger. "Tell me, Sir, who's the fraud and who's the real Mr. Fairfax. Perhaps you could explain this email from Mr. Edward Fairfax."

Eddie stared at the bony hands holding the incriminating evidence and knew if he dared look at the eyes he felt boring into him, he'd probably jump up and run out of this crazy office and keep going until he got to the train station. He felt Vickie lay her hand on his arm.

Nigel was waiting with the estate wagon as Eddie and Vickie climbed in the back seat. Eddie took Vickie's hand, gave it a good squeeze and shook his head – a sign to say nothing until they were alone back at the manor house.

Eddie's thoughts swirled on the short drive back to Fairfax Manor. What had happened? The single sheet that Rhetts had pulled from the file was a hard copy of an email from Edward. His expedited passport had finally arrived, the email had said, and he would be arriving at Heathrow airport the morning of 14 June. If there were no delays, he would call at Solicitor Rhetts' office the following morning at ten a.m. Eddie looked at his watch. Today was the fourteenth.

As much thought as he had given to the day when he would finally meet Edward, the last twenty-four hours had changed things. Now he wasn't so sure that meeting Edward was in his best interest. He was certain he wasn't ready for a personal encounter. What would he say? He was beginning to suspect that he knew what Edward would say once he had seen Fairfax manor, his inheritance. And there was the encounter of over four years before. They hadn't actually met and talked to each other - but they knew each other's faces.

Edward had been less than understanding and really, why was Eddie expecting anything to be different now? Was he just being foolish, indulging in wishful thinking? It was all his own fault, he fretted. He had been so caught up in the travel, in Chalmers' story and in the awesomeness of Fairfax Manor itself that he had failed to monitor Edward's email as he should have. Perhaps for some other reason, Edward had checked his spam file and found this little diamond in all the junk.

"Sorry, Sir. Didn't mean to stop so abruptly." Nigel's worried eyes watched him from the rear-view mirror. The estate wagon had lurched to a halt. "Sorry again, Sir. Guess I wasn't paying proper attention." The stone wall in front of the house loomed large in the windscreen. Another few feet and Nigel would have scored a direct hit. That's ok, Eddie thought. Inattention to detail wasn't just Nigel's problem. Before Nigel could get out and reach for the back door, Eddie turned to Vickie, "I need to take a walk and think this over."

"What am I supposed to do?" Vickie hissed.

"I don't know," he snapped. "Go take a nap, whatever. Paint your toes again, I don't care. I just need time to think."

As Nigel helped Vickie from the car, Eddie swung his legs out and started back down the road through the woods toward the village. He walked until he crested the hill and the road began its downward grade.

He didn't want to deal with anyone else he might meet on the drive and took a path that he'd noticed from the car. It crossed over a fence on a stile and disappeared into the forest. It must be a hunter's path, Eddie thought, although Eddie knew his way around a forest about as well as he did Buckingham Palace.

The quiet of the forest was a good place for thinking, unlike trying to work through a problem with Vickie around. He was surprised by the way she had changed since their arrival in England. He had come to England with the idea of learning something helpful about and from Edward.

Vickie had come . . . well, he couldn't quite decide why she had come. Curiosity maybe. Perhaps she didn't want to be alone in New York. But once she had seen Fairfax Manor, she wanted it. She wanted what Sir Reginald's money could get her. He wasn't sure he liked the new Vickie or the way she was acting. She had goaded him into going back to see Rhetts too soon and he hadn't been prepared for Rhetts' surprise.

He thought he'd handled it as well as possible. If he hadn't convinced old Rhetts that Edward was the imposter and that they would get to the bottom of things when this interloper arrived, he at least had confused matters enough to give him some time to think.

He stopped and sat on a large stone that lay at the intersection of two trails. It was a kind of trail marker, he decided, with yellow and red parallel bars painted on its side. He had to be realistic, he admitted, once Edward arrived, he and Vickie would have no chance of pulling off a claim to be Sir Reginald's heir.

Vickie had awakened him twice last night asking if he was sure he could continue the charade. He would just have to be strong long enough to get past the day, she told him. They'd establish themselves at Fairfax manor, and then they could fire everybody who might ever learn the truth. It was a plan that would work, she had assured him with the strength of someone who had obviously put much thought into the idea. Or, Eddie wondered, was it the assurance of someone who had tried a similar scheme before?

Eddie wasn't as certain. It was an appealing idea to be sure, but his deceptions had always been at arm's length. The shock of Rhetts' surprise made him realize that he hated confrontation and wasn't very good at bluffing his way through difficult situations. He hadn't been in that position since Prestonburg. The thought of that brought an ironic smile to his face. The chief guard at the prison could be a new world incarnation of old Rhetts.

He stood and continued along the trail. Being out in the woods alone with no distractions had helped him focus his thoughts and make a decision. Edward would be here tomorrow and Rhetts and Chalmers would be his allies, Eddie's adversaries. He'd go back and tell Vickie. She'd argue, he was sure, but they'd have to abandon this silly plan. It had never really been workable, only something she had dreamed up after getting to England. He could always make a living doing what he had been doing. He didn't need a lot. He'd be happy just to quit worrying about his problem. Even that didn't seem as important now. That was it, he'd settled it.

It also dawned on him that he had an empty feeling in his stomach. Surprising since he'd had a large, typical full English breakfast. A quick look at his watch explained the reason for hunger. In the deep gloom of the forest floor, he hadn't noticed that the sun no longer slanted rays through the high branches. It was after seven p.m. He'd been walking for hours, thinking, arguing with himself and preparing to defend his decision to Vickie.

He stopped and looked around him at the towering trees, now darker in the receding light. It should be simple, he thought, just turn around and go back the way he had come. He'd tell Vickie his decision, they'd invent some reason to be taken back to Moreton, and be gone before Edward showed up. He was now very sure he didn't want to meet Edward. What could Edward do for him or more exactly what would Edward be willing to do for him once he learned that Eddie had planned to nip his inheritance? Eddie remembered Edward's reaction to his simply pinching a few bucks from his checking account. That reaction hadn't exactly been friendly.

He felt relief for having arrived at a decision. Now he just had to stay resolute enough to convince Vickie that he was right. The shadows in the forest on either side of the trail were now dissolving into each other, trees indistinct against the forest background. The sky that he could occasionally glimpse through the thick canopy was taking on a deeper hue, dotted here and there with a pinprick of a star.

He quickened his pace. He didn't want to be caught in the unfamiliar environment of a forest at night. He had lost track of just how far he had come while he wrestled with Edward and Vickie, and Rhetts. . .and himself. Had he really been wandering the forest path that long? It had been hours.

Another hour passed while Eddie picked his way along the increasingly darker path. His mental processes, now off Edward and Fairfax manor, were concentrated on putting his feet quickly and surely on the path and not on something to trip over or a hole to drop a foot into. Eddie felt a strange relief wash over himself as he regained the drive to the manor. With a pace spurred on by the growing gloom of the forest, he crested the hill and soon saw lights in the manor house windows. Now breathing heavily, he slowed his pace. City life hadn't prepared him for country exertions. He hadn't let himself think about being lost in the forest while he was on the trail, but now he shook off the spooky feeling and relaxed a bit as he walked on toward the lights.

He was ready to drop the big door knocker when a gentle push on the door showed it to be open. The entry hall was almost as dark as the forest but with his eyes now acclimated to the dim light, he navigated his way to the grand staircase and found his way to their room. But the door was locked. He tapped lightly hoping not to gain the notice of anyone but Vickie.

The door immediately opened just enough to see two eyes peering out of the dark room. He pushed in and turned to flip the light switch. He was momentarily blinded but could see that Vickie had been crying. "Where were you?" She demanded. "I thought you had left me here." She threw the dead bolt and grabbed his arm. "I did it." she said. "For both of us."

He looked at the tear-tained face, the disheveled hair and a look he had never seen on her face before. It reminded him of someone waking from a nightmare, unable to understand the difference between dream and wakefulness. "You did what?" he asked.

"It," she repeated. "When you went off walking to think things over, I had Nigel take me back to town and I did it."

He had to tell her of his decision, but he had to get her attention first. "Calm down." He put his hands on both her shoulders. "What is it you did?" he asked again slowly.

"I went to his office and I killed him. Now we won't have to go back to New York. This," her eyes swept the room, "will be ours."

"Vickie, stop it. That's something you don't kid about. Listen to me. I've made a decision."

"I killed Rhetts, Eddie. Now the old man won't be able to give away your inheritance to Edward."

Eddie was sure he had heard her this time but what he'd heard was impossible. He looked into her tear-reddened eyes and a shudder shot up his spine. She was serious. He could barely mouth the words. His tongue and lips suddenly bone dry. "You're not serious. . .you didn't do something insane."

"I had to, Eddie, you were getting weak and were about to give this back. I had to do something. Old Rhetts was going to side with Edward. I did it for us, Eddie."

"Noooo. . . you couldn't have killed someone!" Eddie wailed. "Not old Rhetts, he was just a harmless, crazy old man.!"

"Yeah, and that crazy old man was going to mess up our plans."

Eddie looked at the stoney-eyed person sitting on the bed and suddenly believed her. She had come to desire what wasn't hers more than anything else in the world. Maybe he shouldn't be surprised. He'd only known her for a few weeks and really knew nothing about her other than a few personal quirks.

The sometimes sweet, sometimes moody, always goofy woman he'd shared his life with since coming back from Prestonburg may have just come back from some place equally dreadful. She'd had the instinct to immediately recognize the cops. Maybe this wasn't the first time she had done this, murdered someone. She had just confessed to planning it, confessed the motive, expected it to work out.

Eddie could feel his hands begin to shake. He would admit to being a thief and would even accept part of the blame for that, but to murder someone over money – over anything – was beyond his comprehension. "You've got to get out," his voice was rising, "the police will figure this out quickly. You don't want to go to prison and I'm not going to be a part of this." Eddie knew he could never commit murder but he would be called an accomplice and accomplices went to prison too. "You've got to get out now before they come here."

Vickie gave him a feral stare, "I did that for us, for you, and now you're throwing me out?" she screamed. Eddie clamped his palm over her mouth, "Settle down, everybody will hear you."

She jerked away from his grasp but she was strangely quiet.

"Tell me you're kidding," he wailed, "because if you're not, you're crazy. I'll give you what money I have. Take your passport and head for the airport. Stay in the village tonight, take a taxi to Heathrow in the morning and get out of the country. Now!"

She stood still with her hands on both hips, eyes boring into his, "You're the one who's crazy. You're a coward. We could have all this, but you don't have enough guts to do what I did." Eddie was speechless in the face of this person that he realized he knew nothing about at all.

Vickie calmly opened her suitcase, pulled out her passport and stuck it in her purse. "Ok, give me all the money, I'll need it."

Eddie slid his hand into the side pocket of his suitcase and handed her a stack of both pounds and dollars. He wondered if he would be considered an accomplice for helping her escape. He didn't care. He didn't want to see her go to prison; he somehow owed her his help but she had to be raving mad. "Ask Nigel to drive you to the village. Tell him you left something important at the hotel."

"You'll be sorry, Eddie. I thought you came over here to see this through. You really are a coward."

"Go, before it's too late."

She gave him a last piercing glare and was out the door. Just as quickly and easily as she had come into his life, she was now gone out of it. An eccentric coming in, a monster going out. Had such a change really happened in a few short weeks, or had the monster lived just under the surface all along? He thought about the salamander. He was staggered and overwhelmed at what he'd just heard. He had come to think that Vickie was someone who couldn't step on a bug but then he'd read Edward very wrongly, too. He'd paid for that with four years of his life. He didn't want to pay for this misjudgment with even more of his life.

Who else was he misjudging? Rhetts, probably. But he didn't matter anymore, the poor old man, dead, and for what reason? He shuddered at the thought. Was Chalmers who he seemed, just an elderly caretaker of the estate until the heir was in place. Eddie would love to ask him, but he had been noticeably absent since early morning. In fact, he hadn't seen any staff at all since they had returned from their encounter with Rhetts.

By now, they all probably knew what had happened at the offices of Dunham Solicitors and were avoiding him and Vickie, fearful of this killer in their midst. And if that were true, was the next knock on the door a cop ready to slap cuffs on him?

Eddie stood paralyzed, unable to decide what to do when he heard the faint clatter of a diesel engine. He couldn't decide if the car was arriving or leaving, and what a difference that would mean. He stood so still that the only sound he heard besides the dying away diesel clatter was the pumping of his own heart. And it was dying away, the car was leaving not arriving. Vickie was going, cops weren't coming for him.

Eddie tried to assess his situation. Nothing looked in his favor. Old Rhetts was dead – murdered. Vickie had changed into something horrible, Edward could be there to confront him in the morning, Chalmers - who might be an ally - had disappeared. A grim thought struck Eddie – he felt he had been close to an answer to the question that had obsessed him for so long, and now, so many new questions with no possible answers. He took several deep breaths.

He'd take the questions one at a time, he decided. Edward had an appointment at Dunham Solicitors at ten in the morning. Old Rhetts wouldn't be there . . . but Eddie would.

Chapter Twelve

Chipping Campden

Nigel had driven Vickie down to the village and dropped her at the Lygon Arms. She needed a room, she told the reception clerk, since a family emergency required a quick trip back to the states and she expected a very early pickup next morning by cab. Vickie was surprised at herself, at the way she was handling this situation, thinking things through. She'd never had much confidence in her abilities but it was amazing how murdering someone clarified your thinking processes.

She'd seen Eddie as a smart but troubled person who obsessed over his name, something that didn't really matter. Now when it came to something that did matter, the chance to become wealthy – literally a gift handed to him – he panicked and couldn't make a smart decision. She realized that she could make that decision when she needed to.

When Eddie had gone off alone on his walk to think, she decided that Old Rhetts was the main obstacle that stood between her and Eddie and the wealth of Fairfax Manor. Eddie had told her about his first meeting with Rhetts and how the old solicitor expressed bitterness at the Fairfax family. Then Chalmers told his version of the uneasy relationship between solicitor and client. Then she had finally met Rhetts and seen first hand his perverse joy at flipping around the email and watching Eddie squirm, perhaps a last chance to deal a blow to a Fairfax. She had hated him from that moment.

She hadn't gone to his office with the idea of eliminating him from the equation but to make a deal. Apparently Rhetts had felt shortchanged by Sir Reginald for the whole of his career at Dunham Solicitors and would welcome the chance to have some revenge. Vickie had never had much in the way of possessions but had very quickly recognized the significant difference between being poor and being rich. She much preferred what Fairfax Manor represented. She just as quickly recognized that if sharing a part of that wealth was the way to hold onto the rest of it, then it made so much sense to do just that.

Sitting alone in her room at Fairfax Manor while Eddie was out tramping through the forest, thinking who knew what, she decided that promising a part of the wealth of Fairfax Manor to Rhetts to get him to cut

Edward out was a sensible bargain. She knew that Rhetts was expecting Edward at ten o'clock the next morning so she had to get there before Edward. She needed time to convince Rhetts to become her ally.

She had the feeling the old man would jump at the chance to double-cross Sir Reginald and especially find it appealing to reap some financial rewards in the process, something he'd felt left out on for his whole career.

If Eddie hadn't been so obsessed and had more guts, he too would have seen the possibility in this strategy. It would work, she was certain. She was also certain that Edward was expecting nothing more than the rundown cottage that Rhetts had described to Eddie. If the estate was really worth as much as it appeared to be, they'd just have to keep Edward away and thinking "rundown cottage."

They could then easily peel off a few thousand pounds to satisfy Edward and send him back to America, happy and out of their way. She just had to get to Rhetts before Edward did. Today was the time. She hurried downstairs to find Nigel.

Rhetts had seemed quite surprised to see Vickie at his door when he answered the knock. He said nothing but pulled the door further open as if to say a grudging welcome. "You're lucky to catch me here," he said, "I came in to prepare the papers for the real Mr. Fairfax. He's arriving tomorrow, you know." Vickie could hear the scorn in the wheezy voice. She went in and he closed the door behind her. She followed him into the second office and took the chair he pointed to. He sat behind the big desk with his chin propped on his hands. Vickie knew what she wanted to say but had a hard time deciding where to start. Finally Rhetts grunted and said, "You have something you want to say to me Mrs. Fairfax – if you really are Mrs. Fairfax?"

Vickie caught the taunt in the last words but took her chance to say what she had come to say. "Ok, so Eddie may not be the Edward Fairfax you're looking for but I don't think you really care." She waited for some sign that he was following where she was going. He gave a small wave of his hand.

"Help us, me and Eddie, get Fairfax Manor and part of everything is yours." There, she had laid out the bones of a deal. Rhetts' answer had been quick. He reached for the hand piece of the old-fashioned phone. As he started to dial, he calmly told her that he was calling the police.

She couldn't allow him to do that.

She picked up the base of the phone and swung it in a round-house blow at the surprised old man. A crunching collision to his head was accompanied by the sound of the tinkling bells inside the device. Frightened eyes stared at her for only a moment, and slowly rolled up to expose the veiny whites. Rhetts slumped over in his chair and blood began to freely ooze from a long wound across his forehead. His hand still grasped the receiver. It twitched a few times before the device slid onto the desk.

Now she sat in a darkened room at the Lygon Arms. She thought better in the dark. She had done what she had to do and if Eddie was too weak to see that, he would have to pay the same as Rhetts had done. Vickie listened for the sound of sirens or any commotion indicating something had happened at Dunham Solicitors.

The village lay under a blanket of quiet that she had never experienced in New York nor even suspected existed.

Vickie lay back on the bed in the dark and thought of what she must do in the morning. Eddie had told her to get out of the country. Of course, that would be what he wanted. But that wasn't what she planned to do. It would be days before anybody missed a crazy old man like Rhetts. She'd get to his office before Edward and hide the body in the second office. Then she'd wait for Edward in the first room.

The next morning, Vickie felt refreshed. There was still no unusual activity in the streets. That didn't really surprise her. Even if someone had found the old man's body, they'd never suspect that the person responsible was just in the next town. She was safe in Chipping Campden, but she had to get back to Moreton and be there when Edward arrived.

She hadn't intended to kill the old man, but it was done. He'd threatened to call the police, and she couldn't let him do that. She'd have to tell Edward. He would understand when she told him about Eddie and what he was planning to do; that old Rhetts had conspired with Eddie to take his inheritance. That was right, she told herself, Eddie and Rhetts were working together to cut Edward out. A dead man couldn't argue. She could tell the story to suit her own purpose.

Vickie told the cabbie to get himself a coffee and wait for her. She walked the short distance to the office of Dunham Solicitors and climbed the stairs, listening for any sounds from the office above. There had been no unusual activity on the streets to suggest a crime had taken place in the sleepy little town.

She didn't remember if she had locked the door as she left Rhetts' office but the door gave way to her push. She hadn't thought how she would feel when she walked into his office and saw the old man slumped over in his chair, by now, covered in his own blood. Would she be instantly accused and repelled by that scene? Would she be terrified by what she had done? Would she be able to carry through with her hastily conjured plan or be a coward and weakling like Eddie? If she could pull it off, would it haunt her for life?

She stepped quietly to the door of the second office, so quietly the miniscule squeaks of the wooden floor boards sounded like some primal animal screams. There was too much at stake to go soft now, she told herself.

She started to push the door open to see the terrible scene of an old man lying dead - dead by her hand. But she decided that she didn't need to see that. It wasn't that she had regrets. After all, the old man would have taken away what she had spent a lifetime dreaming about. She never expected to realize that dream but now that it was within her grasp, some old man wasn't going to come between her and a once in a lifetime chance to have everything she had ever wanted. Now she had to be strong and do what she had to do. She'd deal with guilt or whatever it would be later.

She had no watch, but she sensed that the time for Edward's appointment with Rhetts was close. An appointment she would keep for the old man. She would wait at his desk in the outer office, sit in his chair. A plan was quickly taking shape in her mind. She hadn't planned on taking this road when she came with Eddie, but she was now committed and what was to be gained was too great to panic and lose it all. She had never known the possibilities that existed and once she had seen them, she wasn't about to be scared away.

Before the last piece of her plan could fall into place in her mind, a quick three raps came from outside the main door. Vickie rose from Rhetts' chair and purposefully walked to the door. She pulled the door open to find a thin, middle-aged face staring inquiringly at her. He was shorter than she had expected and thin to the point of gauntness. Maybe she had expected him to look something like Eddie, younger and handsome.

"You must be Edward," she said without emotion. The thin face gave a nod. She turned and walked back toward the desk. "Follow me."

Edward followed her and took the chair she pointed to and Vickie again settled into Rhetts' chair.

Edward's eyebrows rose and fell as he took in the ancient surroundings. "You're not Rhetts," he said with the statement hanging in the stale, musty air. "Are you?" he added with uncertainty.

"I'm Vickie. You're here about the will?"

Edward nodded.

Vickie looked at the spare frame and drawn face. Edward's tight grip on the arms of the chair and his hollow eyes gave him the look of someone on the edge, teetering back and forth. Vickie looked at the man across the desk and wondered why Eddie had been so obsessed with the idea of meeting him. She knew she didn't have a lot of time to say what she needed to say. She expected Eddie to be there soon. He wouldn't be able to resist the chance to meet Edward. She decided that she had to be quick. Maybe even a little shock would work in her favor. Vickie stood up and looked down at Edward, "Rhetts is dead. I'm here in his place.

If the look on Edward's face wasn't exactly shock, it was a tense concern, an animal skittishness in his eyes. He started to say something, but Vickie went on.

"I was Eddie Fairfax's girlfriend. . . until he killed old Mr. Rhetts. She followed Edward's eyes. They flicked left and right. He was processing information he hadn't expected.

"I had to warn you." She said. "I couldn't let him do that again . . . to you," she added.

The alert in Edward's eyes now crystalized into fear. He jumped to his feet. "Who are you. . . and who's Eddie?"

"I'm Vickie, like I said, and I think you know who Eddie Fairfax is."

The fear and confusion showing on Edward's face suddenly gave way to a different look as the new information meshed with his memory.

"It can't be. The Eddie Fairfax I know about is in prison. He's a thief. He ripped me off with that ATM scheme of his." Edward looked at the face across the desk. There was no denial.

"Are you telling me that that Eddie Fairfax is here, that he killed the man I was supposed to meet?" He gave a nervous glance toward the door. Suddenly a reading of a will to hand over a simple cottage had turned into something threatening. "Why would he be here?" Why would he. . .kill . . .this person I was supposed to meet?"

"Listen to me, we don't have much time. Eddie plans to kill you too."

Edward glanced from the door to the window as if trying to decide on the best escape. "Kill me? He wants to kill me? Why?

"To keep you from inheriting Fairfax Manor." Vickie said as she watched his eyes. "He wants it and all the money that goes with it."

"What money are you talking about? His voice rising. "The lawyer that called me said it was just a small cottage. I almost didn't come. I don't need some little hut in the woods in England. I live in New York. I have a job there."

"That's what Eddie thought, too, when he read your email," Vickie went on.

"What do you mean, he read my email? I don't remember getting. . .how could he read. . .?"

"At first he just wanted to meet you but when he found out that the 'cottage' was a huge mansion that had servants and lots of land, he decided to take it himself. Old Rhetts threatened to call the police and to tell you. That's when Eddie killed him. It was terrible. The poor old man had no chance, lots of blood and screaming for help." Vickie could see that her story was having the desired effect on Edward. "And now that you're here, Eddie said he's going to kill you, too."

Edward fell back in his chair and stared at the door. He ran long, thin fingers through his hair and turned back to Vickie, his eyes nervously darting from Vickie to the door and back. "This is crazy. Why would he want to kill me?"

"I've just told you. . .to keep you from inheriting Fairfax Manor. That's why I'm here. He tried to kill me too when I told him I was going to warn you. Then he screamed at me and said he'd kill us both. I tried to tell the police, but they wouldn't listen. I think he's got to the local police. Convinced them with a lie or bribed them or something." Vickie watched Edward's eyes. He was believing her. He obviously wasn't used to being told that someone was going to kill him.

"I think it's terrible that he stole so much money from you, but that's nothing if he kills you and takes millions that belongs to you. He shouldn't be able to get by with that." Vickie dropped the word millions into the story and saw a flicker of anger cross Edward's face. His eyes had stopped their bouncing and were now riveted on Vickie. "Did you say millions? So this rundown cottage has not only turned into a mansion but now it has millions of dollars attached to it too? The solicitor said it wasn't worth bothering with. What's going on here?"

"That's what he told Eddie, too, when he thought he was you, but it turned out to be a huge mansion, a bunch of land and the old man Fairfax is loaded. Rhetts hated the Fairfax's. They had been terrible to him and he was just trying to get even. He'd never even seen it. When Eddie saw what was at stake, that's when he de- cided to get rid of me and old Rhetts. Now, it's only you that stands between him and inheriting a ton of money. He's gonna come looking. . ." Vickie stopped and put her finger to her lips as she heard noises in the corridor. "It's him," she hissed to Edward. She knew he would come. He wouldn't - couldn't miss the opportunity to meet Edward. "He's come for you."

Panic gripped Edward. "What do we do?" he moaned.

Vickie stayed calm. She was pleased that Edward had used the word 'we.' "You have to kill him before he kills us." She heard Eddie moving around in the corridor and saw that Edward had also heard his movements.

Edward jumped from his chair and looked for an escape route. "I can't kill someone, not even him."

Vickie knew she had to act now . . . she only had seconds. Edward was being weak like Eddie, unable to make a decision when he had to. She was the strong one and she liked the role. "We'll be partners," she told Edward. "I'll do it. It's either him or us."

Edward looked at her wild-eyed. He stood frozen. She knew he would be no help. She moved quickly to the side of the door and picked up one of the metal bookends off a shelf, books tumbling to the floor as a result. She looked back at Edward who stood anchored to the floor, shock branded on his face.

The door opened slowly and Eddie stood there, staring at the man he'd last seen four years before. The man he had tried to meet, the man he desperately needed to ask a hundred questions. Eddie stood mesmerized. Although Edward had aged a lot in the four years since he'd last seen him, Eddie recognized him instantly.

Eddie had long waited for this moment. There was no court, no judge between him and Edward. He finally stepped into the room, smiled and held Edward's gaze. He held out his hand as he approached Edward. He'd already made the decision that the friendly route was the best way to begin. As he started across the room his foot kicked something on the floor. Eddie looked down and saw a book go skidding across the bare planks. Then Edward disappeared.

The heavy bookend caught him squarely on the side of his head. Blood sprayed from his head and Eddie's legs turned to jelly. The last thing he saw was the salamander leaping at his face. It seemed to have something big and heavy in its mouth.

Vickie calmly put down the bookend and walked toward Edward. Edward's feet had come unglued from the floor and he took a couple of steps back and slid sideways behind the big desk. "You're crazy," he screamed. "Get away from me!"

"It's too late for that," Vickie said. "We're partners now." Edward swallowed hard and coughed as if his last meal was about to come up. He sunk into the old desk chair and started to run his fingers through his hair again. Vickie was getting tired of weak men. She'd have to take control. "Edward, look at me. We've got to get out of here. Where are you staying?"

Edward didn't respond but continued to comb his fingers through his hair. Vickie bent to the floor and picked up the book Eddie had kicked across the room and slammed it down on the desk. Edward jumped at the gunfire-like report.

"Do I have your attention, now?" Vickie said, gritting her teeth.

Edward looked up at the woman with the wild red hair but saw nothing but dead calm eyes, "Get up and let's get out of here," she said. "You can come to my hotel room while we figure this out."

Edward put both hands on the desk and pushed himself up as if his legs had lost their strength too. His gaze darted back and forth between Vickie and the crumpled form of Eddie lying on the floor, blood lazily seeping from the side of his head.

Vickie walked to the door, looked around the corner and motioned for Edward to follow. He moved toward the door but gave Eddie a wide berth. The question showed on his face. Which was worse, going with this crazy woman or staying there with a dead body. He looked at Eddie again and followed Vickie out the door.

Vickie said nothing to Edward on their walk to the Lygon Arms. She was amazing herself with her coolness and ability to think and plan what to do next in tough situations. She knew she needed Edward as an ally and by the time they arrived at the hotel she had devised a plan to convince him that he not only needed her but would probably agree that she had done the only thing that made sense. Eddie had put himself in the way of both Vickie and Edward and this was not the first time that he had been a thorn in Edward's side.

Edward remembered his anger in the courtroom when this crazy guy and his lawyer had tried to make him feel guilty for not being sympathetic. It was unbelievable. A guy steals your money and not only wants your sympathy and understanding but then has the nerve to act hurt and betrayed when you ask for justice. And now, if this woman he was following was right, this Eddie had tried to steal from him again on a much grander scale. Edward was surprised when the thought hit him that now . . .he wouldn't have to ever deal with this Eddie character again. Vickie steered Edward into the pub at the hotel and ordered two pints of ale.

"He was crazy, you know. He was obsessed with you. All he talked about was finding some way to meet you. He thought you could help him in some way." Vickie watched Edward's eyes. He was staring at his glass. She wasn't getting through. "I saved your life, he was going to kill you." Edward's eyes shot up and fixed on her face. Good, she thought, I had to say it again that someone wanted him dead.

"He was going to steal your money again, too. He had figured out some fancy electronic way to clean out your bank account. And of course after he hacked into your email and found out that you had inherited that big mansion, he knew he would have to kill you. Take your money and kill you too. That's what he had planned for you. . . and I saved your life."

From the minute he had arrived in this small village, Edward felt as if he were irreversibly slipping over the edge of a black hole. Things were happening unbelievably fast. He had come to England because an email said he had some insignificant inheritance - probably worthless - and he'd spent money he shouldn't have chasing the crazy idea.

Then when he walks into a musty old office to meet with the solicitor who sent the email, he is confronted by this insane woman who has now killed someone, a woman who claims that his inheritance is worth millions. Then she tells him it was going to be stolen by a scumbag who had ripped him off before and should still be in prison, now on the outside involved in the same criminal activity. Then she tells him this same criminal has hacked into his email account and even wants to kill him. It was getting to be too much, way too much.

The look of fear on Edward's face was changing to one of anger. "He hacked into my email? And he was planning to clean out my savings? Didn't four years in prison teach him anything? The sonufa . . . I should have killed him myself. I couldn't get him out of my life. What did he think I could help him with? Better still, *why* did he think I'd help him. . . after what he did?"

Vickie could see that she was beginning to get through to Edward. But she realized that Edward was weak like Eddie and would need more convincing. She saw how he had frozen at Rhetts' office and was unable to help her. It was a good thing she could act in such situations. "We'll put your bag in my room and then we'll go for a walk."

"What walk? I don't want to go for a walk, I want to get out of here."

"Without your inheritance? We can be partners, you'll be rich."

"You're nuts. Can't you tell the difference between a shack and a mansion? The solicitor said it was probably worth very little and that it was stuck back in some woods." Being angry at this Eddie character was one thing, but chasing around looking for some worthless piece of property with this insane woman was crazy and scary. He should never have come.

"You can't believe him, he's dead." Vickie said sharply. "That's why we're going for a walk. You need to see something"

Edward wanted away from this woman but if the solicitor really was dead, then the trail to his inheritance was just as dead. He'd never been in England before and had no idea what to do. All he had was a name, Sir

Reginald Fairfax. As to the location of the cottage he was supposed to inherit, he assumed it was somewhere in this area called the Cotswolds but, in fact, could be anywhere in England. He wasn't sure what to do next.

What he was sure of though, was that now he didn't care about or even want some worthless piece of property. It would just be his luck that it had a huge overdue tax bill attached to it.

He looked at the henna hair but it was the ice in her eyes that told him that she expected no more argument. Edward picked up his bag and followed her out of the pub. He'd decided he shouldn't argue further with someone he'd just seen bash a guy's head in. What alarmed him more than what she had done was his sense that she had no problem with it and would do it again without hesitation.

He warily followed her to the second floor and set his bag just inside the small room. "I'm supposed to be out of the room this morning," she said. "I'm going to the front desk to see if I can get an extra night. I'll meet you just outside on the street." With her last word, Vickie was already hurrying down the corridor. Edward thought for just a second that he'd forfeit his bag and take the opportunity to get out of the hotel, out of Chipping Campden, and away from this crazy woman.

Edward couldn't explain to himself why, but he stood waiting outside the hotel door when Vickie came out.

She led him on the now-familiar route. Past the Eight Bells Inn, the alms houses, and the old Wool Church of St. James. Charged with adrenaline, Vickie was walking at a fast pace, looking over her shoulder every few steps, ready to grab Edward and disappear off the side of the narrow lane should she hear a vehicle approaching.

"Look, I can't keep up this pace. Slow down." Edward was breathing heavily.

"Come on," Vickie pointed to the obscure lane that left the road they were on and climbed the hill into the woods. As soon as they were off the main road, Vickie stopped to let Edward catch his breath.

"This road goes up and over that hill and ends at Fairfax Manor, your inheritance."

"This cow trail? Edward kicked at a lump of earth and sent it flying into the grass. "You're trying to tell me this road leads to a mansion?

Vickie glared at him. "Just shut up and stay with me." She started off up the earthen track at a fast clip. Edward struggled to match her pace and barely noticed when the forest closed in on the track from both sides. He was breathing heavily, sweating profusely, and watching the track at his feet to keep from stepping into a rut and walked right into Vickie. She had stopped. "Sorry," he said between breaths. He noticed that they were now at the top of the hill and saw her pointing ahead. He looked to where the trees were now falling back from the widening lane. The grand, three story building filled most of the horizon.

"Holy shit! What's that?" he gasped between breaths.

"Fairfax Manor. . . .that's your inheritance."

Edward turned to look at Vickie. His mouth hung open and he was still breathing in short, rapid gulps. He mumbled something Vickie couldn't hear but finally managed to say, "You're crazy. Why are you doing this?"

"I'm not crazy, that's it . . .that's yours. . .that's your inheritance. It's ours," she added.

He stood panting and looking. He finally regained his breath and in a raspy voice said, "That's really not a cottage, is it?" A grin began to form on his lips. "You are nuts if you're telling me that's mine. I don't believe it. Why are you doing this? You killed that guy Eddie and dragged me up here for a joke."

She looked at the manor for a few seconds and turned back to him, "Yes, it is yours, but only if you've got the guts to fight for it."

Edward decided that whatever she was up to it wasn't a joke.

Vickie suddenly grabbed his arm and pulled him towards the trees.

"What are you doing," Edward howled.

"I hear someone coming. Quick, let's get into the trees."

They lay hidden in the tall grass that grew between the first line of trees and the road. The vehicle was moving at a fast speed for the condition of the road and accelerated when it reached the graveled stretch near the manor house.

"That's the manor's estate wagon," Vickie said to Edward. "Something's going on or Nigel wouldn't be driving that fast. Let's get out of here and back to the hotel. We'll figure something out."

Edward looked back at the grand building and seemed mesmerized, unable to move. "Come on," she said sharply, grabbing again at his arm.

Chapter Thirteen

Fairfax manor

E ddie touched the side of his head and felt something sticky when he rubbed his fingers together. He vaguely wondered if it had anything to do with the roaring noise and pain in his head. He slowly tried to open his eyes. The light hurt and the two figures swimming around in his blurred vision made little sense. A soft hand was gently wiping his forehead with a warm cloth and murmuring soothing sounds. He tried to sit up but the soft hand gently pushed him back. A deafening crescendo of the roar in his head also said that sitting up was a bad idea. Eddie waited until the roar and the pain had settled down and slowly opened his eyes again. The soft hand belonged to Evie who was wiping blood from the side of his head. Chalmers' head filled the rest of his vision.

"How are you feeling, old man?" Chalmers sounded worried. "Someone seems a bit upset at you. But we've had a doctor look you over and he thinks you'll be fine." Eddie didn't feel fine, but appreciated the encouragement.

"Here, take this." Evie held out a couple of pills and a glass of water. "The doc left this for you. Strong stuff, he says, so it should help the pain." Eddie slowly swallowed the pills and felt as if gravel from the drive had gone down his throat. He coughed and felt the roar start again.

"Easy, old man, you should be feeling better in just a moment," Chalmers said as he dragged a chair across the floor.

Eddie finally sat up with Evie's help and without too much increase in the pain. Good medicine, he thought. His vision was slowly clearing. Chalmers pulled the chair to where he faced Eddie. "I sent Nigel to pick up something at Rhett's old office and he found you in a dreadful heap on the floor. He brought you back here. You've been out for some time. Good to see you finally come around. You had us worried."

Eddie looked from Evie to Chalmers and back to Evie, who still had a look of concern clouding her pretty features. Funny, Eddie thought, he hadn't really noticed before just what she looked like. She always seemed to be hidden in the shadows. And Nigel could have left him there in old Rhetts' office and let him die or Chalmers could have refused to take him back in if he knew what had happened at Rhetts' office. They probably did know, he worried, and thought he had something to do with what happened to Rhetts.

Eddie looked at Evie and Chalmers again. "You know what happened at Mr. Rhett's office?" Both nodded. "I had nothing to do with that." Eddie admitted to himself for the first time in his life that he was a thief. But he hoped with all his being that he could never be a murderer. "Vickie wanted me to kill Rhetts so we could take Edward's inheritance away from him. But I couldn't do something terrible like that. I didn't know that she could do that. . . that she did that. . .until she told me. Said she did it for us." A low, mournful sound came from Eddie's throat. The thought that someone had killed - thinking it was for his benefit - frightened and distressed him beyond his ability to reason it through.

"After Vickie saw Fairfax Manor, everything changed . . . . Vickie changed. She decided that somehow we had to take this away from Edward. She wanted to get back to Rhetts' office and sign whatever papers we had to before Edward got here. She was only thinking one minute ahead the whole time. When we got to Rhetts' office, he said he'd found out that I was a fake. . . or I think that *fraud* was the word he used. He actually asked which one of us was a fraud, me or Edward, but I knew who he meant, because. . . I'm the fraud. . .

"We came back here and I wanted to give up the idea and go home. I needed to take a walk to clear my head. While I was out walking, actually getting lost in the forest, Vickie went back and that's when she did it. She killed Rhetts and came back and said she had done it for us. I couldn't believe what she was saying. I told her to get out. I gave her all the money I had and told her to get out of the country. I didn't want to see her go to prison."

Eddie looked again from one to the other, "I've been there – in prison, but maybe you knew that already. Again Chalmers nodded. Before it would have worried Eddie that Chalmers seemed to know so much about him, but now, he didn't care. He was finished with this insane idea.

"After she left," he went on, "I decided to go to Rhetts' office to meet Edward and apologize to him for all the trouble I had caused him in the past." Eddie started to explain but Chalmers raised his hand, "We know all about that, too."

"Anyway, I did. I went to Mr. Rhetts' office when Edward was supposed to be there according to Mr. Rhetts and there he was. Just standing there. I know he recognized me, but he didn't say a word. I was going to shake his hand and tell him how sorry I was and then. . .

"Something came crashing down on your head." Another voice, another figure suddenly emerged from the shadows and filled Eddie's still shaky vision.

"Rhetts!" Eddie shouted and tried to stand up but his legs wouldn't respond. A ghost! But he didn't believe in ghosts. Was he going mad now?

"You're not dead!" he finally managed to whisper, hoping it was possible.

"No," The old man smiled, "just the victim – or perhaps I should say the beneficiary – of an inept killer just as you were. We know you had nothing to do with this."

"Rhetts, I think we should tell young Eddie what's going on here," interrupted Chalmers. "He certainly deserves some answers after what's happened."

Rhetts nodded.

"Old Chalmers died about three years ago." Chalmers said as he gave Eddie a sly smile and waited for his reaction. "He was my butler, and a fine one at that." Either Eddie was a bit slow in grasping what he'd just heard or he was just beyond any further shock. He simply looked at Chalmers with a blank expression.

Chalmers went on. "Rhetts and I were sitting here before the hearth in this very room last winter enjoying a glass of whiskey and talking about the old days. . .er. . . that is, when we were working together. One of us said – and I don't recall which – that it was a bloody shame that Fairfax Manor would too soon be going to the government since I was the last of the Fairfaxes and getting on in years." Chalmers stopped and watched Eddie's face and laughed as he realized that Eddie had finally registered his earlier remark about Chalmers dying and that he was the last of the Fairfaxes. But the increasing look of confusion on Eddie's face said he needed a clearer explanation.

"That's right, I'm Reginald Fairfax, not Chalmers. He's already passed on, rest in peace. We miss him terribly. Isn't that right Rhetts?" Rhetts nodded with a doleful look. Sir Reginald took out a handkerchief and dabbed at his eyes.

"Now, let me get on with my story." But Sir Reginald stopped again and turned toward Evie. "Evie, dear, would you be so kind as to bring us some of my favorite whiskey and some glasses. I think young Eddie could benefit from a good stout drink and I don't imagine that it would hurt Rhetts and myself either." Sir Reginald gave a low, rumbling chuckle. After Evie was out of the room, he turned back to Eddie, "She's Chalmers' grand-daughter and a good girl."

Eddie nodded his agreement. She certainly had a gentle touch.

"Well, as I said, we were sitting here lamenting the fact that Fairfax Manor would someday soon belong to the government blokes in London. Then Rhetts brought up the second son business. Rhetts, I believe, told you about that." Eddie started to nod again but quickly decided that it felt better for his head just to utter a raspy 'yes' with his dry lips and tongue.

"At any rate, it sounded like a capital idea to try to find out if there might be an heir in America who could help me cheat the government out of a few thousand acres and a big house for at least another generation. I asked Rhetts if he would take up the challenge of finding that relative." Reginald looked toward Rhetts and smiled. "He's quite good with a computer, you know. We worked together at MI6 during the Cold War. Been friends ever since." Reginald again noticed that a lack of comprehension showed on Eddie's face.

"MI6 is Her Majesty's equivalent of America's CIA."

Eddie blinked his eyes.

Rhetts took up the story. "I found two . . . two Edward Fairfaxes that might actually be true descendents. And it turns out that your father was one of these second sons of a second son, making him, in fact, Sir Reginald's cousin. The 'second-son' business ended long ago but it seems that it's still used as a rationale by some young men to trudge off on their own adventures, or in some cases an excuse for ne'er-do-wells. At any rate, your father came back to England from the U.S. some thirty- five years ago to try to reclaim his heritage. He seemed to accomplish little more than spawning several illegitimate children and absconded back to the States when the father of one of the girls declared his intent to make a gelding out of him. As far as I could determine, your mother was the only one he actually got around to marrying. Sir Reginald was delighted to have at least two candidates."

"Yes, delighted," repeated Sir Reginald, who antici- pated Eddie's next question. "The reason your own fa- ther wouldn't be the more natural heir is simply the fact that he seems to have totally disappeared. If he's still alive he's most likely still in hiding from the one father, the one who promised to cut off his balls." Sir Reginald looked at Rhetts, slapped his hand down on his knee and laughed until a coughing fit stopped him. A final cough and he cleared his throat.

"Well, at any rate, Rhetts and I decided to have a little contest between the two Edwards and have a little fun in the bargain. We made up the whole story about the squabble between my old man and Dunham and between Rhetts and myself." Sir Reginald smiled at Rhetts, "We spent many a pleasant evening right here before the fire over the course of the whole winter. We put quite a dent in my stock of Macallan 25 while we laughed and made up different plots to our story. We had a grand old time and we knew all we had to do to set things in motion was to send Rhetts' email to Edward.

"Our private investigator in New York had learned enough about you to know that you would be all over that message. Sir Reginald looked at Eddie and smiled evenly as if he knew the question in Eddie's head, "Why, the very thought of Rhetts and me feuding is ridiculous. We've been friends forever."

Eddie nodded.

"And of course, once the game was started, we had to decide what parts we needed to play. Rhetts could be himself and if I had already passed on, I had to be someone else. So I thought it quite appropriate to give dear old Chalmers another go at it.

And quite naturally, Evie would still be my, that is Chalmers' granddaughter. We thought it would be interesting to see how you two would react to the story and perhaps that would tell us something important about the two of you, which one might be more deserving of winning our little contest."

"That part about the 'cottage'. . .", Eddie croaked.

"Oh that," laughed Sir Reginald, "that was all Rhetts' idea. I had never heard Fairfax Manor called a cottage until you and that woman came 'round asking about it."

"Imagine," added Rhetts, "if I had put the words 'inheritance' and 'manor house' in the same sentence there would have been a stampede. I wanted our game to develop at its own pace. I didn't count on that woman changing all the rules."

"You know," Sir Reginald said, "it gets harder for old men to have fun." Rhetts and he looked at each other and chuckled. "Rhetts was able to verify that you really are related but hasn't been able so far to do the same for Edward. There were a couple of missing pieces in his puzzle but we decided to give him a chance since you were

such a scoundrel with your thievery and prison record."
Sir Reginald said the last, not with the slightest hint of
malice, but simply as a matter of fact. Eddie didn't feel
insulted and certainly couldn't argue the point.

"As of our last communication with Edward, we were
expecting him yesterday. But since, as you well know,
Rhetts was *dead* too, we couldn't very well send him to
meet Edward. If you and Vickie had seen him, our game
was up. We especially wanted to know how you'd react
to her smashing poor old Rhetts over the head." Sir
Reginald turned toward Rhetts, "I do apologize for that,
old man. It wasn't a part of our plan." Rhetts grinned
and waved a hand in dismissal.

"I sent Nigel to meet Edward instead," continued
Sir Reginald. "Regrettably, he had a flat tyre on the estate wagon and was late – got there in time to find you
bleeding all over Rhetts' floor. Whoever did that to you
was already gone. And if Edward had ever been there, he
was gone too. We had to assume that your bashed head
was also courtesy of your Miss Vickie and that Edward
had for some reason gone with her."

Reginald halted his story as Evie returned with a
tray. She put the bottle of single malt on the table by
Sir Reginald and handed one glass to him and one to
Rhetts. As Reginald poured three fingers into his own
glass, Evie went over to Eddie and put a glass on the
table in front of him and then touched the side of his
head. "That feeling better?" she asked softly.

"Yes, thank you." Eddie said looking up and trying
to smile.

"Thank you, Evie." Reginald said and Evie took her
cue to leave the room.

"After what she's done," Eddie said, "I wouldn't call her 'my' Vickie."

Rhetts grunted and touched the bandage on his own forehead, "I completely understand your sentiment. That woman is. . ."

"I know," said Eddie. "I've only known her for a few weeks and just thought she was a little nuts. . .you know, nuts like strange. I had no idea she could do this. I've never seen anyone change this way."

Rhetts picked up a folder from the table, took out a sheaf of papers held together by a paper clip and handed it to Eddie. "Read the first page of this. It's the summary of a report prepared by our private investigator in New York. The investigator had originally been engaged to build a file on you but then Miss Vickie came on the scene and we asked him to include her." Rhetts looked toward Sir Reginald who took up the story.

"Turns out," Sir Reginald said wryly, "that she was the interesting one." Reginald nodded at the papers in Eddie's hand. Eddie brought the top sheet closer to his eyes to compensate for the dim light. The shock of what he read must have shown on his face as he looked up at the two older men.

"See what we mean?" Rhetts said.

Eddie looked from one to the other. Could this be another little wrinkle in their old man's contest? No, the look on the two faces told him that what he had read was true. It was unbelievable but actually made sense when he thought about it.

"After seeing this report," said Sir Reginald, "Rhetts and I thought about letting you in on what we had learned but decided not to."

"Quite right," said Rhetts, "we thought two old government operatives could keep everything under control; that what we'd found out just added an extra dimension to our game."

"Excuse me gentlemen, I think I hear the phone," Sir Reginald said. Eddie thought his ears were the source of the ringing but watched as Sir Reginald opened the lid of a small writing desk and lifted the receiver off an old-fashioned telephone like the one in Rhetts' office. Sir Reginald answered with "Fairfax Manor" and listened with an increasing look of concern taking over his features. After a minute, he put the receiver back on the base and closed the lid of the desk. He turned toward Rhetts and Eddie. "I'm astonished, he said shaking his head. That was that Miss Vickie. She wants to come to Fairfax Manor; she says we need to talk." Reginald rubbed his chin, "She said it would be a very bad idea for me to involve the police."

Chapter Fourteen

Chipping Campden

'Unbelievable' was the only word that kept running through Edward's thoughts as he and Vickie kept up a quick pace down the drive from Fairfax manor toward the village. Was the old solicitor who'd contacted him about the inheritance so stupid as to think this place was a cottage or just maybe he had told Vickie the truth, he'd never actually seen it, never been invited to the Fairfax mansion.

Vickie had told him about the long feud between the solicitor and the Fairfaxes and Edward could understand why. Now, he was beginning to think it more likely that the old solicitor was in league with that Eddie character. He'd probably do it as a way to get even with Fairfax.

Edward had been angry enough when that thief Eddie had stolen his money four years before, but seeing him get his due in court and knowing that he was sent away to prison was a sweet revenge that took some of the sting out of his loss. But now he was back and interfering in his life again, brazenly trying to steal from him again.

As the anger welled up in Edward, he thought for a moment of what Vickie had done. He knew he couldn't have harmed Eddie, much less killed him; the thought of it almost made him ill. But he had to admit that since it was done, he wasn't going to shed any tears. He wouldn't ever again have to deal with this thief. He was a determined SOB, fumed Edward to himself and this time he even had an accomplice, a woman who was just as crazy as Eddie was determined.

Vickie kept looking back, ready to pull Edward away from the track and into the trees should Nigel or anyone else come along the road. She had no idea how much Chalmers might know and she didn't want to get into a conversation about Eddie and Rhetts.

Vickie and Edward reached the edge of Chipping Campden without passing any traffic. They retraced their path by the church, along the little street of the alms houses and by the Eight Bells Inn.

"We're almost back. Are you hungry?" she asked Edward.

He'd been thinking about Fairfax Manor all the way back, but now that she had mentioned it, yes, he was hungry. Edward wanted to say 'after what you've done you feel like eating?' but the empty feeling in his stomach simply made him nod yes. Only two of the tables in the pub had diners still eating their way through a late lunch. A couple of business types stood at the bar finishing off their pints.

Vickie led Edward to the booth by the front window where she could see anything going on along the high street. She put a fifty-pound note on the table by Edward. "You have to go to the bar to order. I want to keep an eye on the street. Just get me the daily special."

When Edward came back from ordering, Vickie took her attention from the street and concentrated on Edward. Nothing was going on that she could see out on the street, just lazy local traffic. Maybe no one had found Rhetts or Eddie yet. The way that old office looked, it might still be days before anyone wandered up those steps and found them. Good, she thought. That gave her time to think of something else. She wasn't going to leave empty handed. She had come too far and done too much. She knew exactly what that meant.

Her thoughts were interrupted by the waitress with their food. Both she and Edward quickly tucked into the big plates of bangers and mash. Their walk had worked up strong appetites for both. They ate without talking. Finally, Vickie stabbed her fork at the last piece of sausage on her plate and looked up at Edward, "He was crazy with the idea of getting even with you."

"Getting even? What are you talking about? I haven't done anything to him."

"You sent him to prison." Vickie replied coolly, watching Edward's eyes.

"He sent himself to prison." Edward had laid down his fork, his voice rising.

"Keep it down," Vickie said sharply, "You want everyone in here to hear you?"

He leaned closer, "The guy's crazy. He stole not just from me but from a lot of other people and he went to prison for that. And he blames me? That's nuts."

"Maybe so, he was going to kill you and I saved your life. He said he'd kill you the first time he saw you."

"You're as crazy as he is. . . was. How are you going to explain away two murders?" Edward glanced around the pub and leaned in toward Vickie again, "And you still think you're going to claim this inheritance?"

Vickie didn't answer. She needed time to figure that out. She was confident that she'd think of a plan. She was proud of the way she had handled herself the last few days. She could see that Edward had been affected by seeing the manor. She recognized the look on his face.

Once he had seen the wealth sitting right there in front of him, he couldn't get back to the 'cottage in the woods' indifference. He'd never be able to walk away as if he hadn't seen it. She just had to find a way to make this happen and she would have an ally. She had to make him think 'we.' Fairfax Manor was so different from the idea of going back to that tiny apartment in New York.

"Look, never mind that I saved your life, you know you want this as much as I do. I've never had anything in my life and I'll bet you're the same."

Edward stared at her as he chewed but didn't argue with what she'd said.

"You haven't done anything wrong so far. I need your help, so stay with me. If something goes wrong, no one will blame you. If we get lucky, well, we both win."

Edward looked warily at Vickie, "You're saying you'd take all the blame yourself? Why?"

"I want this more than anything in my life."

Edward still looked unconvinced when Vickie saw it out of the corner of her eye. Fairfax Manor's estate wagon had just gone down the high street and Vickie was quite sure it was Nigel at the wheel.

She grabbed Edward by the hand. "Let's go. I have an idea."

Edward followed Vickie along the broad high street of Chipping Campden. She looked right and left until she finally spotted it on the street across from a small car park. The manor's estate wagon was parked in a loading zone; apparently Nigel didn't expect to be gone long. The exhaust system was still clicking loudly as it cooled. Vickie motioned Edward to stand with her on the passenger side until Nigel came back. Within a couple of minutes he came out of the small grocery shop carrying a folded newspaper under his arm and crossed to the driver's side of the wagon.

Vickie pulled Edward around the back of the wagon to meet Nigel just as he arrived at the driver's door. "Nigel, this is a friend of mine. We would like a lift back to the manor house." She opened the back door without waiting for his answer. Nigel looked at her, at Edward, and shrugged, "Of course ma'am."

As Nigel executed a u-turn in the street, Edward squeezed Vickie's arm and said through clenched teeth, "What the hell do you think you're doing. We can't go back there."

She turned to Edward and buried her nails in his arm. He let go of her with a little yelp. "Shut up and back me up." She let go of his arm and began digging in her purse. When the estate wagon had cleared the edge of the village and turned on the road behind St. James Church, Vickie pulled a cylindrical shape from her purse and shoved it into the back of Nigel's neck.

"I've killed Eddie and I've killed Rhetts," she said to the startled driver, "and I'll kill you if you don't do exactly as I say." Nigel's hands flinched on the wheel and he braked to the side of the narrow country lane.

"Turn the wagon around and take us to Gloucester or I'll blow your head off." Vickie's voice had a chill in it that had Nigel turning around without argument.

"What do you think you're doing," Edward hissed in Vickie's ear. He looked at her hand resting at the base of Nigel's neck. The car bounced wildly as Nigel executed a quick turn at a rutted pull-off. Edward couldn't quite make out what Vickie had in her hand, but he thought it looked like a bottle of nail polish, the long, round lid pressing into Nigel's flesh. Edward was beginning to regard Vickie now with real fear and was surprised when he experienced something else, a grudging admiration.

After the first shock at having a gun pointed at the back of his head, Nigel decided she wouldn't kill the driver with the wagon hurtling along at fifty miles per hour. "Why are you doing this?" he asked.

"Eddie and I were going to inherit Fairfax Manor but he was a coward. He couldn't go through with what it took to get it. I had to kill him just like I had to kill old Rhetts. And now, Edward's my partner."

Nigel didn't understand exactly what she was talking about but a sudden thought made him start to feel bolder. A look in the rearview mirror at the face of

Vickie's companion wasn't much help. The man's face had a look of anger but the eyes darted back and forth with fear. A tiny seed of an idea, an old personal agenda, began to resurface in Nigel's mind. If he could somehow make himself valuable to this crazy woman it might work. "How are you going to explain two murders?" he began.

Vickie was getting tired of this question. She shoved the bottle harder into the back of Nigel's skull. "I won't have to," she said. "Now I have a hostage. I wonder how much you life is worth to Chalmers."

"Who's Chalm. . . ? Nigel decided to go straight to his point. "What if I could help you?"

Vickie kept the pressure on the bottle and gave a little laugh, "you are helping, you're my hostage."

"No. . . I mean I could pretend to be your hostage . . . but I could help."

"Why do I need your help? You'd just want part of the ransom. I'd be crazy to agree to that. The answer is no. She gave a sharp push to the bottle. Nigel flinched again but wasn't going to give up on an opportunity he'd never expected to have again. If he let it get away now, the chances of a second shot at his dream were probably less than zero. It was a chance to get back to Belfast and work again with his IRA cronies trying to get the bloody English and their influence out of his country. He needed money for that, a lot of money.

"Just listen to me." He kept one eye on the road and the other on the crazed woman with the red hair that filled his rear view mirror. "I need money to get out of this country and get back to Ireland. I can help you. I don't care a bloody damn about Fairfax Manor or the bloody old Englishman. Besides, I know something you don't. It'll make a big difference. It'll make the difference between you getting the ranson money and not getting it." He added as an extra incentive, "Wouldn't it be better to have me on your side than having to worry about me escaping or something. . .? Two head's are better than one; that sort of thing."

Vickie's hesitation gave Nigel a little hope that she was really considering his idea until she said, "I'd just shoot you if you try to escape. I'm already in so much trouble with killing two people, and now kidnapping. I'll kill you without worrying about it. If you don't cooperate. . .you're dead."

"You're not in as much trouble as you think you are. Make me a partner and I'll tell you what I know. Believe me it changes everything. Are we partners?"

Vickie got a firmer grip on the nail polish bottle, "I should just pull the trigger and end this now." She watched his eyes widen in the rear view mirror and then squeeze shut, "watch the road, you idiot. Ok, we're partners. Now pull over and tell me what you know that's so important."

Nigel braked hard to be able to stop at an upcoming turnout. He set the hand brake and looked up at the rear view mirror, "Old Rhetts and your husband aren't dead, just a few cuts and bruises."

"You're lying to me," Vickie snapped, as she gave the bottle a sharp thrust.

Nigel winced, "easy with that thing. I'm not lying. I found Rhetts lying in his office and carried him back to Fairfax Manor. Today I was sent back to his office to pick up some papers and there was your husband, same shape. I carried him back. Two days in a row Doc Steadwell's been called out to visit the manor.

"Evie came down to the kitchen just before I left. Picked up a bottle of the old man's favorite whiskey and three glasses, loaded it all on a tray and left. Now who else could all that be for, I ask you. Rhetts, the old man, and your husband." Nigel was proud of his deductions. Vickie started to tell him that that worm Eddie was not her husband but let it go.

"Who's Chalmers?" Vickie asked.

"Chalmers," Nigel repeated, shrugging his shoulders, "he was the butler, but he's been dead for a while, maybe two or three years. The pretty little thing, Evie, she was his granddaughter."

Vickie considered what Nigel had said. It answered a couple of questions that had been bothering her.

"Where could we get a hotel close by?" she asked. "But not in this village."

"Moreton-in-Marsh is the closest town and it has a few hotels." Nigel answered.

"Take us there. We'll get some rooms and figure this out." Vickie took some pound notes from her purse and reached across Nigel's shoulder, "Then dump this thing and go rent us another car."

His experience in Irish Republican militias had taught Nigel the value of a strong command structure and if they got out of this, he was going to try to recruit this woman. Edward sat quietly beside Vickie in the back seat and looked at her with awe.

Nigel dropped the shift lever into 'drive' and started for Moreton-in-Marsh.

Chapter Fifteen

Fairfax Manor

Sir Reginald, still in the persona of Chalmers, waited for Evie to show Vickie into the Hunt room. It had been a good half hour since she had called. When the entry bell rang, he sent Rhetts and Eddie down to the kitchen. They all felt, that no matter what she wanted, it would be better if she didn't see the two she thought she had so recently dispatched.

Vickie stood in the doorway. The quiet and slightly goofy girl that had shown up at Fairfax Manor with Eddie only a few days before was nowhere in evidence except for the red hair. There was the cool, calculating countenance and ice in her eyes that completely made him unaware of the hair. Sir Reginald turned to face her squarely, the thought that he didn't want his back to her unnerved him.

"I'd offer you a seat and something to drink, but I take it this isn't a social call."

"No," she said evenly as she came further into the room.

"And just what is it I don't need to involve the police with," he asked as evenly as he could despite the fact that his pulse was racing to the point that he could feel it in his temples. It was a feeling he hadn't experienced since MI6 days.

"Edward and I have your driver, Nigel. I killed Rhetts and I killed Eddie and I'll kill Nigel if you screw this up in any way. If you don't do exactly as I tell you to do . . . your Nigel will die."

Sir Reginald felt a chill crawl up his spine and a gut feeling told him he'd encountered no one like her since his 'working' days. Even though he knew that Rhetts and Eddie were alive and well down in the kitchen, to hear someone confess to murder so easily and coldly shook him. It didn't bode well for Nigel, either.

"You have two days to have two million dollars and one million pounds. I'll be back to collect it and if you try to involve the police, I call Edward," she nods toward the cell phone in her hand, "and Nigel dies. It's that simple. Do you understand?"

Sir Reginald had thought he could defuse this absurd situation after she had called but now he was stunned at the change in this woman, a cold-blooded presence he could actually feel, like the uncomfortable cold sweat that dampened his palms. He recognized the cell phone she held as an old one he'd given to Nigel to stay in touch when he was out in the estate wagon. He didn't doubt that she was telling him the truth. All he could do was nod to her demands and try to figure something out when she was gone.

She held up the phone, "Exactly twenty-four hours," she said. "Have it ready." Sir Reginald stared at the back of the departing Vickie and thought how the red hair made him think of the devil.

He was still shaking after he'd called Eddie and Rhetts back from the kitchen. He repeated what she'd told him and her demands. He looked from Eddie, who had taken up his position on the divan again while he rubbed his head, to Rhetts. "Looks like our little game has got out of hand, old chap and I'm not sure what we can do about it. I worry for poor old Nigel, he's not much of a brave soul. I feel responsible since we've cocked all this up."

"No sir, It's all my fault." said Eddie. I didn't start out planning to do it, but I let her convince me that we could somehow pull it off and take Edward's inheritance. I came to England just to meet him and see this place. I really hoped that coming here would answer a lot of questions for me. Then it turned into more, we got greedy. I'm sorry, I really am. I just thought he could help me with something, but that doesn't matter anymore. I don't want his inheritance. I just want to go home and try to straighten out my screwed up life." Eddie began again to carefully massage the side of his head around the bandages.

Rhetts walked to the divan and laid a thin hand on Eddie's shoulder, "The inheritance is actually yours, not Edward's. We didn't communicate with you directly because I knew you had already hacked into Edward's email account. We wanted to see what you would do. That became part of the little game."

Eddie stopped rubbing his head and looked up, a puzzled look on his face. Sir Reginald laughed dryly. "He's quite good," he said sweeping a hand toward Rhetts, "having spent several years at MI6. While you were snooping on Edward, we were snooping on you."

Eddie slowly took this in but wasn't surprised. At this point, he felt beyond surprised. "And I'm really sorry at what you must have seen," he groaned. "I've let *my* life turn into a miserable wreck and me into a miserable person and I sure didn't know she was like this, I mean, that she could try. . . even want to kill somebody. I'm sorry I brought her here. I've been so stupid and worried so much about something that really doesn't matter." Eddie rubbed his head again and winced when he touched an especially tender place. And what he'd just heard himself say seemed as if someone else had said it, but it was true, he knew it was really true – and it really didn't matter.

The name business he had worried about for so long was foolish. It was a non-issue. A sense of enormous relief washed over him and brought an involuntary, choking laugh. He looked up at Rhetts. "She's crazy but I don't want to see her go to prison. Rhetts, you and I are still alive so she hasn't really murdered anybody and if we promise not to turn her over to the police, she may be willing to let Nigel go. If she sees us when she comes back it might shock her enough to give up this insane idea." Eddie found himself pleading for the sake of the old Vickie.

Sir Reginald and Rhetts looked at each other. "That makes some sense," Sir Reginald said.

"I don't quite remember which of us actually came up with this idea, this game thing," said Rhetts, "but we've opened old Pandora's box and I feel quite responsible."

"Amen," said Sir Reginald, "but what to do about it, that's the thing!"

"You and I are alive and agree to keep the police out of this whole thing," Eddie said, "but there's Nigel and the kidnapping. Even if she lets him go, he may not be willing to agree with us.

"Well, assuming we get him back safely," Rhetts said, as he thoughtfully rubbed his chin, "Nigel may not be a problem. He doesn't know that we know, but he's been a person of interest with the authorities in Belfast for years. He's kept himself out of trouble by living quietly here and been a good employee so we saw no need to cause him any problems. Any notoriety from this might bring people here he wouldn't want to see."

"It would certainly bring people and publicity I wouldn't want for Fairfax Manor," agreed Sir Reginald.

"I have something else I have to tell you." Eddie looked distraughtly from Rhetts to Sir Reginald. "I gave her several thousand pounds when I sent her away. She and Edward could last out there for a long time and since you say we can't ask help from the police we have no idea where they might be. She could be holding Nigel anywhere in the Cotswolds."

"That's a good point, my boy," said Sir Reginald, and if she's told him that she's killed you both, the old boy might just panic and lose hope; might try to do something stupid and get himself killed."

"But he knows that we're alive; he carried us both back to the manor himself," Rhetts protested.

"But if you'd looked into her eyes . . ." said Sir Reginald, "she thought she'd killed you both and had no problem with it. That's certainly convincing enough for me." Sir Reginald shook his head, "Look at what we've done, Rhetts,"

Eddie continued massaging his head. Sir Reginald now looked about the room wondering if Evie might have left the bottle of single malt handy.

Rhetts smacked his thigh with a palm, "By George, I've an idea. Just might work and have a little fun to boot."

Sir Reginald's attention was back on Rhetts and Eddie watched as the old man's eyes lit up.

"Here's what I propose," Rhetts said. His voice had a seriousness about it, but the mischievous look on his face told Eddie that the old man wasn't quite ready to give up on his game yet.

"We'll have the room very dark and young Eddie and I will dress up like ghosts when Miss Vickie comes back and scare her into giving up her plans. After all she thinks we're dead, right? Could be fun."

"Are you guys serious? Eddie jumped to his feet. "She could flip out and do something awful. That's a really crazy idea,Eddie said.

"He's right, Rhetts," Sir Reginald said. "That's a bit over the top. I think we've had our fun but now it's gone all sour. We have to find a way to make this end well."

"There's only one thing to do," Eddie said, "let's be honest with her." Rhetts and Sir Reginald glanced at each other. "Go on," said Rhetts.

"I've already said it. If all three of us are here when she comes back, she will see that no one's been killed. She won't be charged with murder and can still walk away. If you're sure that Nigel will be willing to forget, then she can leave with all the money I gave her and she can make a new start for herself. Just free Nigel, and go! That's what we tell her."

"What do we do about Edward," asked Rhetts.

"That's easy," replied Sir Reginald, "he can leave with Vickie if he wants to or I can just declare him out of the game. . . disqualified, as it were."

—

Chapter Sixteen

Fairfax Manor

E ddie wasn't looking forward to seeing this new Vickie. He'd never figured out the old one, and was still shocked by the person who walked with a newfound and cold confidence into the Hunt Room the following day. The strange aura of menace that accompanied her pervaded the room. It occurred to Eddie that they could have set a clock by Vickie's arrival – exactly twenty-four hours to the minute. Rhetts, Sir Reginald and Eddie expected a shocked reaction from her when she saw the two she thought she had killed. She walked right past Eddie and Rhetts without a word or glance.

She stood facing Sir Reginald. "If these two are still alive, "she jerked a thumb back in their direction, "then I'm not surprised to see you are too, Chalmers. . . or should I say Sir Reginald". Surprised and helpless looks ricocheted between the three men.

"Where's my money?" she said in a voice that was low but infused with steel.

Sir Reginald swallowed hard and looked at Eddie and Rhetts. "Young lady, it's true that I am a man of some means but getting together that amount of cash in a day is not something even I can easily do." He was stalling and hoping for some further inspiration.

"As you can see," said Rhetts, "young Eddie and I are quite alright save a few scratches and bruises and willing to let past insults be forgotten if you just let Nigel go free. You can take the considerable amount of cash young Eddie gave you and depart our fair country."

Vickie glared at them, especially Eddie, "Screw you both. You shouldn't be alive." She turned back to Sir Reginald, "So. . . where's . . . my . . . money?"

"So," he repeated, "I don't have it and you don't seem shocked to see them."

"I found that out from Nigel. Hold a sharp knife to his throat and he tells everything he knows."

"You can't do that," Eddie stepped forward, "Just release him and get out of the country. You don't have to go to prison."

"Shut up, you coward," she spat the words at him. Pulling the cell phone from her pocket she dialed a number and coldly gave a command that sent another shock wave through the room. She then put the phone on speaker and held it up for them to hear. A blood-curdling scream vibrated the small device.

She had told Edward to amputate Nigel's thumb and send it to Fairfax Manor as a little incentive to getting the money together. She thrust the phone in Sir Reginald's face and hissed, "Now, you've got one more day. Screw this up and Nigel comes back piece by piece." Vickie was out of the room like a cobra recoiling. They knew she'd strike again. They were stunned to silence by what they'd heard.

"You know, as much as we need to do so," moaned Sir Reginald, "and we need to do so more than ever, we can't call in the police, not now. Because we've let it get this far, I'm afraid we'd be considered complicit with this crazy creature. There seems to be no choice but to pay her and pray that we get poor Nigel back safely. I'll call my broker in London; he'll be able to help."

Chapter Seventeen

Moreton-in-Marsh

Vickie tapped rapidly on the door three times. The voices on the other side went silent as someone approached the door. "Who is it?"

"It's me, you idiot." Vickie said just loud enough for Edward to hear a foot away on the other side of the thin hotel room door. The knob began turning and when he was sure it was her, Edward opened it wide to let her in.

"Who'd you think it was?" she asked.

"Just not taking any chances." He looked toward a small side table where Nigel had a deck of cards spread out. A half burned cigarette hung between his lips.

"I'm tired of cards and tired of waiting," Edward said. "What happened? Did you get the money?"

"No, he claims he's having some trouble getting so much so fast. We'll get it, though, so don't worry about that. You should have seen their faces when he screamed." She nodded toward Nigel and said, "Pretty convincing." They believe we're going to slice you up piece by piece if we have to. We ought to send them a package . . .wrap up something, put it in a box and leave it at the front door. They'd never unwrap it. Probably just go bury it," she laughed.

"But don't worry, we'll get the money. They even looked disappointed that I didn't faint when I saw Eddie and old man Rhetts back from the dead."

"Told you my information would be worthwhile, didn't I?" Nigel said. "Tell you something else. The old man, Sir Reginald, is really loaded. If you have them scared enough, maybe we can up the price for my freedom." He laughed as he jammed his cigarette stub into an overflowing ashtray.

"If you don't quit that crap, you won't live long enough to need more."

Nigel ignored her and reached for his cigarette pack, realized it was empty and threw it back on the table.

"Like I said, he's practically made out of money. His old grandfather, like a lot of the English at the time, went off to Africa looking for adventure and treasure. He worked in the Kimberley diamond fields in southern Africa and met another Englishman by the name of Cecil Rhodes. He hit it off with Rhodes and went on to make a fortune in the mines." Nigel was still searching his pockets for more cigarettes. "I just need enough of that diamond money to get me back to Ireland. We've got some unfinished business and the buggers in Belfast seem to be asleep, doing nothing to get rid of the bloody English. With a little of the old man's money old Nigel can get things humming again. All I need is about a million pounds." He grinned, "Wouldn't that be bloody ironic. Using an Englishman's money to kick the bloody English out of Ireland." He had to admire his own brilliance.

"I thought all that was over," Edward ventured.

"It's never over," Nigel shot back. "Never will be."

Vickie stabbed her finger into Nigel's chest. "Listen, I don't give a shit about the idiots in wherever it is you're dying to get back to. Keep your mind on what we're doing here. We need to get this finished and get out of here. I gave them one more day. Tomorrow, we get our money and each of us goes our own way." She looked from Nigel to Edward. Both nodded agreement. Neither felt like spending another day with her.

"Unless you want to stick around and go for the whole thing," she said mockingly to Edward. "Get your inheritance."

"Well, thanks to you I'm screwed out of that," Edward shot back with equal sarcasm, "I don't think I'd be welcomed at the manor with open arms after this." He absently picked up one of the cards from the table and turned it round in his fingers and made a decision. "I'll be happy with my million. And if that boyfriend of yours thinks I was tough on him before, just wait until..."

"He's not my boyfriend," Vickie cut him off. "He's just a weakling like you. Just what is it you're going to do?" she continued her taunt.

Edward glared at her but held his tongue. He'd seen how volatile she could be. And the fact that she didn't seem bothered in thinking that two men were dead by her hand *did* bother him. He'd have to watch her. One more day, a million dollars and he was headed back to the USA.

He looked over to where Nigel was still absently pushing cards around on the table and wondered what Nigel's role had been in the violent past of Northern Ireland. Edward still couldn't believe that only one week before he had been sitting in a small cubicle in New York doing an insignificant job and day dreaming about what his inheritance could be.

Now, any chance of that had disappeared and he was sitting in this drab hotel room with two nuts involved in kidnapping and fraud, attempted murder and who knew what else. He could make it until tomorrow he told himself.

One thing he would not do, though, was turn his back toward this crazy woman.

Chapter Eighteen

Fairfax Manor

Ablack mood hung over the Hunt Room as Sir
Reginald and Rhetts nursed their glasses of
whiskey to steady their nerves. None of them
had slept, the specter of Vickie's return putting a rough
edge on every nerve. Eddie paced the room, repeatedly
stopping to pull back the heavy draperies to see if any
vehicle had pulled into the gravel drive. It was almost
twenty-four hours since she had given her ultimatum
and Vickie would be there at any moment demanding
her impossible ransom.

Sir Reginald's banker in London had just called.
"Sorry, it would be impossible," he had said again, "to

assemble such a large amount of cash under the stipulations that Sir Reginald had set forth." Such an amount would be sure to draw the attention of financial authorities and perhaps even the police and press. "Would a lesser amount be sufficient until different arrangements could be worked out?" the banker had asked. That might be possible in another two or three days. The banker wasn't going to be much help, Sir Reginald had decided.

Eddie heard a car door slam and hurried to the window. A cab sat parked with its front pointing down the drive, apparently ready for a quick departure. He turned to tell Rhetts and Sir Reginald only to see Vickie already standing in the door to the Hunt Room. She ignored Eddie and looked from Rhetts to Sir Reginald, both men staring into their whiskey glasses.

"You don't have the money," she said matter-of-factly as if she had expected it. Sir Reginald nodded. She flipped open the phone and dialed. "It's me. They're stalling us. Do you have a box big enough to hold his hand? Send it to them, now." A pitiful scream shrieked from the phone.

"Vickie, you have to stop this," pleaded Eddie. "I started all this and it's my fault. Take me in Nigel's place and let him go."

She spun around and fixed a tight gaze on Eddie. He was shocked at what he saw. A look of mortal anger bored into him. He instinctively took a step back and averted her gaze.

"So you'd step in for dear old Nigel and risk dying if this old bastard keeps screwing with me? You'd do that?"

Eddie hadn't actually thought about it in those terms, but again made eye contact. "Yeah, I'll go in his place." *Maybe do something decent in my life for a change*, he thought.

She narrowed her eyes as if considering what benefits such a proposal might have.

"Not a chance," she finally said, "but you really are a fool."

Eddie unwittingly dropped his gaze to the salamander. It lay perfectly still.

She turned back to Sir Reginald. "This is final. I will be back tonight. If all the money isn't laying on that table," she pointed to where the empty whiskey glasses now rested, "Nigel will lose one last body part. His head."

She slid from the room like an apparition.

"I'm so sorry I brought her here. This is awful. She was ok - sort of – before we came here. But when she saw this," Eddie spread his hands and looked around the room, "she must have decided she wanted it at any cost. I can't believe anyone could change that much."

"Really?" said Sir Reginald. "Look at you."

"What?" said Eddie, confused.

"Up until a few days ago you were ready to steal what you thought was someone else's inheritance and just now you've offered to put yourself in harm's way for another person, a stranger." Sir Reginald's look said he had seen something different in Eddie.

"Amen," agreed Rhetts.

Both men paced the room and finally Rhetts stopped, "It occurs to me that we may be missing something. Did either of you notice anything odd?"

"Well no. What was it?" asked Sir Reginald

Eddie looked at Rhetts, "The scream, you mean?"

"Right on. A little quick, don't you think? It's almost as if it were planned," said Rhetts. "Staged, so to speak."

"She saw how shocked we were yesterday and maybe she decided to dial up the drama as a way to finally force you into meeting her demands," Eddie reasoned

"What are you two getting on about?" asked Sir Reginald.

"The scream on the phone. It came as if on cue," Rhetts said. "No delay. There was hardly time for Nigel to hear and react that quickly."

Eddie remembered the day he had first met Vickie and witnessed her pitched verbal battle with the landlord. Maybe it was just an act, her way of trying to get something she wanted so badly.

"You may be right," Eddie said to Rhetts and then turned to Sir Reginald. "If you're not going to be able to get the money by tonight, what are you going to do?"

"If this is all staged, it changes everything," said Rhetts as he started pacing the room again. He came back to the table with the whisky bottle. He poured himself another two fingers worth. "She's smart enough to know that if the money wasn't here this afternoon, it won't be here by tonight."

"So what's she after?" asked Sir Reginald.

"Sorry, I can't help you with that," said Eddie. "She never seemed to think that far ahead before and now. . . I don't . . ."

"Let me see if I understand what you two are saying," said Sir Reginald. "You think Nigel's damage was staged; he's faking it. That would mean that Nigel has gone over to the other side."

"Well, we do know he was quite a rabid activist in all the violence that went on in Belfast. Maybe he sees this as his big chance to get back there and take up the cause again. That's why the strange demand as to the ransom - two million dollars and a million pounds. The pounds would be for old Nigel," said Rhetts.

"But what if the whole thing is not staged," Eddie tried again. "I'm starting to believe she would do whatever she thinks she has to. I don't want anybody to get hurt. Especially, since this is all my fault."

"Well, I can't get the money on time and we can't bring in the police. . . and we really can't bring them in now. What are we to do? If this is real, she'll kill him for sure." Sir Reginald stood up and began his own pacing about the room, but stopped in mid-stride, "There's only one thing for it," he said, "we go back to the original plan."

Eddie and Rhetts stopped in their tracks and looked at Sir Reginald.

"And what's that?" asked Eddie.

"Our game," he said, his eyes squinting in thought, long dormant MI6 strategies coming back to life.

Sir Reginald's face wore a vague smile as he laid out his plan and told Rhetts and Eddie their parts in his scheme. Then he picked up the glass from the table and threw back the rest of his whisky. "That's for the nerves," he said, wiping a corner of his mouth with the back of his hand.

"No," Eddie said. "You can't be serious. I agree she's gone mad but she's not stupid. You can't fool her that way. She'll just call Edward and then we all have Nigel's blood on our hands."

"But not if Nigel's become a part of her plot," insisted Sir Reginald.

"We don't know that he has. What if Rhetts and I are wrong about that? If they'd just cut my thumb off, I'd scream just at the sound of the phone ringing," Eddie implored.

"I understand your feelings, but we must have a plan. We have to do something," Sir Reginald's face took on a sorrowful but determined look. "You saw what she was like just moments ago when we couldn't give her what she wanted." He closed his eyes and thought about what he'd just witnessed. "Bluff or not, I've no doubts she would do what she threatened to. And Nigel . . ." Sir Reginald threw out his hands and turned to face the fire. "I'm afraid we have to assume that Nigel has become her accomplice. We've always worried that he'd return to old habits given the opportunity. And she's absolutely volcanic!"

"He's right, Eddie," said Rhetts, "there's no way we can meet her demands by tonight and we can't call the police. On the one hand, if Nigel hasn't gone over, he'll certainly be in mortal danger. You saw how capricious she can be. But if he has gone over, he won't be in danger. Either way, if we bring the police in now, they would likely have as many questions for us as for Vickie. We could be accused of obstruction and endangerment . . . perhaps even being her confederates."

"Did you think of that when you started this crazy game of yours?" Eddie snapped. "You're thinking about yourselves instead of Nigel."

Rhetts and Sir Reginald looked at each other without an answer. "What do you suggest we do?" asked Sir Reginald, chastened.

Eddie began pacing again and ran his fingers through his hair, "Sorry. I don't have an answer either." He stopped at the window and pulled back the heavy drapery for the umpteenth time and froze in place. "They're here. It's Vickie. . . Edward's with her."

Sir Reginald glanced at Rhetts and turned toward Eddie, "It's game time," he said like a man just out of options.

"It's all we have," said Rhetts.

Chapter Nineteen

Fairfax Manor

Rhetts sat bent over in one of the large leather chairs facing the dancing flames on the hearth. He sipped sparingly at his whisky and felt strangely exposed at having his back to the door, knowing that someone who had tried to bash his head in once would walk through the door in seconds, perhaps willing to try it again.

"Where's the money?" Vickie asked without preamble and in a tone that sent a shiver up the old man's back even when he had expected it. "I told you this afternoon that this is my last time to ask. We have Nigel buried." She looked up at the old clock on the mantle. "He has enough air for about another fifty-five minutes. Unless we get the money and get back and dig him out, he's dead. Do you understand that, you old fool?"

Rhetts slowly turned to face her and saw a man, presumably Edward, standing by her side and wearing a similar, half-crazed look. Rhetts conspicuously pulled a handkerchief from his jacket pocket and began dabbing at his eyes.

Vickie's eyes darted left and right around the room. "Where is everybody?" Where's Eddie and Sir Reginald?"

"Young Eddie's gone to fetch the doctor." Rhetts said with as much gravity as he could.

"Why," growled Vickie.

Rhetts dabbed at both eyes again and nodded his head at the large divan across the big room. "Over there, that's Sir Reginald." Rhetts coughed and put the handkerchief back into his pocket. "It shocked him so when you cut off Nigel's hand that he started having chest pains.

'They got worse over the night and just minutes ago the poor sod apparently had a heart attack. Dead in minutes. Now you really have killed someone. I had a devil of a time getting him up onto the divan and now," Rhetts put his hand over his chest and gave a long rumbling cough, "I'm having some pains myself."

"You're lying," Vickie shrieked as she took quick strides and stood by the white sheet that covered the bulky figure on the divan. She reached for the sheet but hesitated and looked back at Edward who uttered a low moan as he ran both hands through his hair. She turned back and lifted the sheet. Sir Reginald lay stretched out with his right arm laid peacefully across his chest, his eyes staring at the ceiling. Edward's moan had risen into a feral scream, "What are you doing? Leave him alone! Let's get out of here!"

She dropped the sheet to hide the accusing look and turned back to Rhetts. The phone in the desk rang which seemed to startle Edward and stopped Vickie in mid-stride. Rhetts opened the desk top and picked up the receiver. After three or four seconds he answered, "Certainly, inspector, we'll expect you shortly."

"You were right, Rhetts," said Eddie, "I can see him well enough through the kitchen window. It's Nigel and he's in the driver's seat." Realizing that the kidnapping had indeed been staged and that Nigel was not only in no danger but in fact was an accomplice in the feigned kidnapping, Eddie sighed as he listened to Rhetts addressing him as 'inspector' and worried what Vickie must be thinking and what she might do as instinctive reaction. Rhetts was obviously enjoying his conversation with the imaginary policeman.

"Of course, inspector, thank you, he'll be sorely missed. Yes . . . we'll see you momentarily."

Then Eddie remembered that she might try to salvage her ruined plot with some revenge. He'd learned the hard way that Vickie strongly believed in 'getting even.' With one of the people who had frustrated her plans lying *dead* in the very room, she would be tempted to finish off Rhetts. No witnesses.

The thought occurred to him that the last witness to her crime would then be himself. One against three. Even so, he needed to get back to the Hunt Room in case he was right. Rhetts would need his help. Since his own greed had caused two old men so much trouble in bringing Vickie here, he would stop it now whatever he had to do.

Then his worst fear was realized when he heard the anguished cry come through the phone and then a long moan from Rhetts. Eddie ran from the kitchen, along the corridor leading to the main house, up the stairs behind the dining room just in time to see Vickie and Edward running out through the entry hall.

He ran for the Hunt Room where the last cries of Rhetts had come from. He quickly looked around the huge room and saw the crumpled form of Rhetts lying on the floor in front of the fireplace. Eddie ran to the old man and knelt beside the helpless looking figure. He quickly looked for wounds or signs of life. Eddie gingerly touched the old man's jugular, checking his pulse. Rhetts opened one eye and gave Eddie a pleased-with-himself grin, "Are they gone yet?"

Eddie jumped back, "You scared the crap out of me! I thought she had really killed you this time."

"Sorry, but when she started toward me with that wild look, I decided to have my own heart attack. It worked. Edward started screaming for them to leave and they took off. I dare say that will be the last we see of that bunch. Help me to my feet, if you don't mind."

As Eddie pulled him to his feet, Rhetts called out across the room, "Reginald, you ok under that sheet?"

Sir Reginald raised the arm folded across his chest and pushed the sheet off. He sat up. "My, my, that was quite exciting. Remind you of the old days at MI6, Rhetts?"

"I do think that of all our games, this was certainly the best," agreed Rhetts. "Splendid finale!"

Eddie looked at them both, Rhetts dusting himself off and Sir Reginald reaching for the whiskey bottle, "I'm glad you're both ok, but this game of yours has to stop. Eventually, somebody's going to get hurt." He saw Rhetts touch the wound on his forehead. "You're right," Rhetts said, "this got quite out of hand. But, all's well that ends well. Wouldn't you say?"

Eddie couldn't necessarily agree but still felt a great sense of relief. "I'm really sorry I brought all this trouble on you. I never should have let her come. . . I never should have come myself. The whole reason I had for being here was insane." He thought again about his name. He no longer cared and suddenly wondered how something so unimportant had gained such complete control of his life and what the cost had been.

A name was just so many words. A fleeting sense of loss became the smallest smile. A twinge took hold, he thought of the word *liberated*. There was no turning back to the old Eddie. He felt an urgent need to get on with whatever his life was to be.

"I've got to get back to New York and figure out what I'm going to do with my life. Or maybe I'll try London. I'm not sure which place is home for me now. I've got a lot of things to think about but I've found at least one answer." An unfamiliar sense of peace had settled on Eddie as he started to stand up. It was time to tell Rhetts and Sir Reginald goodbye.

Chapter twenty

Fairfax Manor

"Sir," an alarmed voice shattered Eddie's newly peaceful reflections. It was one of the assistants from the kitchen. "Nigel and that lady with the red hair made Evie get into the car with them. They were hurting her."

"Oh no," Eddie groaned. Rhetts slumped into one of the big chairs.

Sir Reginald began wringing his hands, "I promised old Chalmers that I'd look out for the girl. And now this devilish woman's taken her."

"That evil woman is absolutely determined not to leave without something," Rhetts said, pounding his fist on the chair arm. "Hang it all, Reg, we've got to call in the law now. This is totally out of control. If they harm that sweet girl, I'll never forgive either of us. Our game is over. We must call the constable."

Sir Reginald was slowly shaking his head, "No, Rhetts, we're past that now. I can't allow scandal to visit Fairfax Manor." He hesitated as if fighting some inward battle, "I'd almost forgotten . . . but there is a way."

Eddie and Rhetts looked at each other, wondering what was going through his mind. Was it another scheme or just a variation on this one?

"And you're right, Rhetts, she is determined to take something away from all this, so she'll be back. I think I know what she wants."

Sir Reginald slowly walked to the tall bookcases that lined the room and moved the ladder to a position to the left of the fireplace. He took hold of the handrail and climbed up to the last rung. His unsteady hand roamed over the highest row of books he was able to reach. He hesitated over one or two of the volumes but finally found what he was searching for and pulled the hefty volume from its place. He teetered for a moment as if about to fall but righted himself and wobbled back down the ladder to the floor.

He turned, looked up at Eddie and Rhetts and laid the substantial volume on the table next to the whiskey bottle. "I'd completely forgotten about this," he said sadly. "It took Chalmer's little girl being in danger to jog this old man's memory." He picked up the book and blew the dust from the top and started to flip open the cover when the phone rang from the inside of the desk. He looked up again at Eddie and Rhetts. "That was fast," he said as he laid the book back on the table and opened the desk. He took the phone from its cradle and put it to his ear and listened to Vickie's latest, and what she said was absolutely her last, demand.

"If you want this girl back alive, there are two things I want and I want them tonight. I've been patient but now that's over. Do you understand, old man? Nigel was right. You two old fools have been playing games with me. Now that's over." Vickie's voice had more steel in it, razor sharp steel. Sir Reginald nodded his head. He had a suspicion of what she was going to demand and now was surprised she hadn't asked for it before.

"I want the book and we want that coward Eddie. Edward and I both have unfinished business with him. You're going to pay and then he's going to pay for screwing all this up. At nine o'clock I want both or at nine-o-one Evie will die a terrible death. You can say goodbye to her now if you're thinking of crossing me again." Sir Reginald heard the phone being shifted and then heard a sobbing plea, "Please help me."

"Are those evil people hurting you, dear girl?" Sir Reginald rasped into the phone before it was jerked away from the terrified girl. "That will be the last time you hear her voice if . . ."

"Ok," Sir Reginald said into the receiver. "Be here at eight and we'll do as you say but please don't hurt the poor girl."

"No, we won't be there at eight." Vickie's voice had a finality that stung Sir Reginald. Had he become confused about her demands in the terror of the moment. Would a misunderstanding on his part doom Evie? He worried.

Vickie brought an icy clarity, "Eddie will bring what I've asked for and meet us at the end of the dirt track where it meets the road to the village. And I don't think I have to remind you again about police. You've waited too late for that haven't you, Sir Reginald? Now, you can't, it's too late. You'd have too much explaining to do." Vickie's voice was taunting. "And you thought I believed your little bit of acting. Nigel said you two had an obsession with games. I see where that creep Eddie gets his weirdness. He probably *is* the real heir." Sir Reginald winced as Vickie cut the connection.

Sir Reginald looked at the two faces watching him, waiting to hear the worst. "I can't do it . . . "his shoulders fell, "but I have to," he said as he tried to work out his frustration and anger by throwing his glass into the fireplace. The crash of glass against the ancient stone startled them all. He picked up the book he had taken down from the shelf before Vickie's call and looked at Rhetts and Eddie. "You're right. We didn't fool her one bit. She wants this," he said holding up the book.

Rhetts nodded and asked, "Nigel?"

"Quite right, it was probably Nigel. Always was the nosey one. Probably planned to steal it himself if he ever got the chance. But how would he have known about it?" asked Sir Reginald.

"Hmmm," said Rhetts. "I think everyone in the house has heard the rumor . . . the legend. Looks like Nigel might have taken it upon himself to learn a bit more than most."

"What are you talking about?" asked Eddie.

Sir Reginald laid the book carefully back on the table and lifted the front cover and motioned for Eddie and Rhetts to approach the table. Eddie saw that the book was hollow and contained a white linen bag that filled the entire cavity.

"This is the endowment fund for Fairfax Manor, or 'rainy-day' fund as my old great-granddad called it," said Sir Reginald, "and what that woman has demanded." He lifted the bag slowly from the book and placed it on the table. From the way it sagged in Sir Reginald's hand, Eddie could see that it was quite heavy. Sir Reginald untied the cord that held the bag closed and pulled open the top. Even in the dimly lit room, Eddie could see the flicker of the fireplace reflect off the exquisite and brilliant glitter of hundreds of diamonds.

"Are those real?" Eddie gasped.

"Not only are they real," said Sir Reginald, "they are of the very highest quality. At today's values . . .

I suppose . . . worth more than Fairfax Manor itself."

Rhetts stared at the fortune on the table before him. "I'd heard the rumor, Reg, but dismissed it as so much local gossip. Every old house has its stories. But this surprises even me."

"Why," was all that Eddie could think to say.

"Besides being very rich, my old ancestor was very practical. When he had Fairfax Manor built, so many of the large manor house owners were beginning to have a difficult time with the awful expenses of running these massive houses. Although that wasn't a problem for him, he looked down the road a few generations and worried that that very thing could happen to one of his descendents. He didn't want Fairfax Manor to fall into the hands of the tax people or his heir to have to do other unseemly things to make it financially."

Sir Reginald idly put a finger in the mound of stones and stirred, causing a kaleidoscope effect, tiny rainbow-like reflections across his wrinkled face. "Having been in the diamond business, he naturally decided that this was the safest and most liquid means of providing for the future security of Fairfax Manor." He gave the bag a little shake and retied the cord. "I suppose I haven't taken this down from the shelf in a decade or so."

"How'd you remember which book it was in?" asked Eddie, surprised at Sir Reginald's ability to recall a book's location after so long a time.

Sir Reginald lifted the book's cover to expose the title. Eddie and Rhetts leaned closer to look, *Cecil Rhodes: Man and Empire Maker*. The author was a Catherine Radziwill.

Sir Reginald looked at Eddie. "There's a lesson in this book for you, young Eddie. The woman who wrote this biography - a Polish princess - stalked, aggravated and sued Rhodes into an early grave. Sounds a frightful bit like Vickie." He grinned, "At any rate I could never forget that title."

"And you're willing to give that up to save Evie?" Eddie asked incredulously.

"Yes, of course, I am," said Sir Reginald solemnly. "Chalmers was my friend and I promised him I'd take care of the girl." Sir Reginald looked toward Rhetts for support. "But I'm afraid this is not the only price for Evie's freedom. The other part's not up to me."

Eddie looked from Sir Nigel to Rhetts. "What else could she possibly want?"

Sir Reginald took a deep breath and pinched the bridge of his nose between forefinger and thumb. "She wants you. She says she and Edward have unfinished business with you. They both seem to insanely think they would have succeeded in gaining possession of Fairfax Manor but for you. She demands that you bring the diamonds alone to where the track meets the main road, the place where you two first came up. Of course we can't ask you to do that."

"Why not?" asked Eddie.

Sir Reginald glanced at Rhetts who had a worried expression. "I'm afraid they mean to do you some real harm."

"I agree," said Rhetts, "other than being cheated on by a spouse, revenge for a loss - real or imagined - is one of the world's favorite motives for murder."

"And you think they really believe they've lost this because of me," Eddie said.

Both Rhetts and Sir Reginald nodded.

Eddie looked at the two old men. Then he thought about the smooth hand that had so gently washed the blood from his forehead. He remembered Evie's fretting over his pain. He couldn't remember when anyone had been concerned for him. "I'll go," he said resolutely.

"We can't ask you to," said Sir Reginald

"I know," said Eddie calmly. "I want to. . . I have to." He looked straight into Sir Reginald's eyes, "But you weren't willing to give up your diamonds to save Nigel when you thought he was in danger."

Sir Reginald suddenly looked at the floor and began re-adjusting the fireplace tools in their stand. Eddie looked toward Rhetts who just as suddenly had begun flicking at something on his sleeve.

Eddie glanced at his watch, "It's half past eight. I'll need to go now."

Sir Reginald turned back toward Eddie and started to object but a quick glance in Rhetts direction affirmed they had no choice. Rhetts nodded at Sir Reginald as he shook Eddie's hand. "Good luck, young Eddie, and do be cautious." Sir Reginald sighed, picked up the book and closed its cover over the bag. He handed it to Eddie. "My boy . . . bring the dear girl back," he said, his voice a strained whisper.

Eddie walked out the huge door he had first passed through just a few days before. So much had changed, he thought, but perhaps too little. In the late dusk, he looked up at the trees on either side of the track, eerie shapes against a darkening sky. He heard the crunch of his steps in the gravel drive finally give way to silence as he came to the soft earth of the track.

He quickly arrived at the part of the track where the trees seemed about to close in from both sides and squeeze the path out of existence and Eddie wondered about his own continued existence. An icy finger seemed to touch his back.

He looked at his watch only to be reminded that his was the cheap kind without a light – useless in the dark. He picked up his pace remembering that Vickie had lately developed a keen sense of punctuality and wished that he'd remembered to bring an electric torch. He twice stumbled in the dark and came near to dropping the book and its priceless contents. He thought of her threat to Evie and his mind lingered for a brief second on what Vickie might have in mind for him.

He couldn't think about that. Evie was depending on him although she couldn't know that her life was in the hands of someone who, only a few days before, would have taken the ransom he carried and left her to her fate. Rhetts and Sir Reginald were depending on him also for their own reasons. And as Eddie hurried down the black path, he realized that he was depending on himself for something he wasn't accustomed to expect. He was expecting Eddie Fairfax to succeed at this mission, something done for another's benefit, not his own.

He felt the grade ease under his feet and realized he was already starting to descend the hill. In a few minutes, he'd soon be walking by the old gatehouse where he and Vickie had rested on their first visit to Fairfax Manor. Suddenly, the sharp outline of its roof rose ghostlike against the blue-black sky. Good, he thought, relieved, he'd be on time.

He also heard a thump in the dark. He stopped abruptly and was immediately awash in light. A car's engine rumbled to life and the headlights began a wild bouncing dance. Startled, he realized the vehicle was barreling toward him across the rutted ground from behind the ruined gatehouse. The awful truth dawned on him - Vickie and her accomplices had never intended to let him reach the road. They couldn't risk having another car pass by and witness whatever they had planned for him.

The sudden appearance of such intense lights blinded him and in a split second the car was so close Eddie could feel the vibration of its engine. He leaped aside just in time to avoid a crushing impact.

Eddie instead impacted something large and extremely hard and solid. His ribs suddenly felt on fire.

He had landed on the large stone where he and Vickie had rested on their way up the hill. The driver was now backing the vehicle to catch him squarely in its headlights. He felt something warm running down his face, a familiar sensation since he'd known Vickie. The car's passenger door flew open and a figure jumped out and rushed in his direction. The moment the figure reached the beam of the headlights, he could see the wild red hair. He felt around in the grass for the book he had dropped on impact with the limestone block. Vickie clicked on an electric torch and waved the beam across the area, past Eddie and finally settled on the book. She bent and picked it up and then walked the two or three steps to where he lay.

She looked down at Eddie, her mouth a hard cruel line, and raised the long barrel of the heavy aluminum torch over his head. He tried to roll out of the path of the descending weapon but, too late, realized that his leg was wedged under a corner of the huge stone. He was able to move just enough to deflect the torch and heard the crash when metal and glass smashed into the limestone.

With her weapon shattered, she used what she had available, a swift kick caught Eddie in the solar plexis. It was a glancing blow but hard enough that he was instantly breathless, his chest on fire, lungs paralyzed, unable to avoid the next blow. Another swing of her foot caught Eddie squarely in the groin. Lightning exploded through his entire body, searing pain ricocheting from one extremity to another.

"I'd kill you if I had the time," he heard her bellow above the roar of his screaming nerves.

Please be quick, he thought.

He'd failed Rhetts, and Sir Reginald and he'd failed himself and most horribly and sadly. . . he'd failed Evie.

Vickie's gaze turned from the helpless figure writhing on the ground to the heavy book she held. She hesitated for an eternity in Eddie's estimation and then turned and walked away. The car was already lurching down the track as she slammed the door. Eddie had tried with all his strength to say, "Let Evie go!" but a gurgle was all that came from his mouth. He watched as the brake lights flashed on. The car had gone no more than twenty meters.

She's coming back, he thought. She's decided that she does have the time after all. She was going to kill him. He tried moving but not a single muscle would respond. *No more kicks*, he prayed.

It was the driver who jumped out and opened the back door. He pulled someone from the back seat and shoved the figure brutally into the ditch at the side of the track. Eddie tried again to call out, "Evie."

Doors slammed, brake lights went off and the car roared on down the track. As the electric blasts of injured nerves in his chest began to subside and let him catch his breath, he rolled over in the dark and slowly pulled his leg from the wedge where the stone met earth. He placed his foot against the stone and gently pushed. No more lightning shot up his leg. It wasn't broken. He tried to stand but a wave of dizziness and nausea flooded over him. He lay back in the darkness and waited for the feeling to pass, waited an infinity for the retching impulse to exhaust itself.

When the spasms finally passed, he pulled at the stone to right himself and wobbled to his feet. He turned in the direction where the figure lay. It wasn't more than a few yards away. He called out, "Evie." There was no response but there was no volume in his voice either. She probably hadn't heard him. His breath was coming easier now as he navigated his way along the rutted track.

He thought he must be close when his foot caught on something and he went sprawling to the ground. He cried out as his damaged ribs jolted him with another electric shock.

It was the figure that was thrown from the car but it had not moved nor made a sound at his contact. He crawled back. The shape in the grass was human. It was warm. And it hadn't moved.

Eddie picked himself up and knelt over the dark and ghostly shape. "Evie," he whispered. He could barely see that her head lay to his right. He placed his hand at the base of her head and searched for the jugular vein, praying to find a rhythm of heart beat. He found the jawbone and lowered his finger to find the vein. He touched it but felt no pulse. He felt sick again as his fingers touched the warm stickiness of blood. Then he felt the stubble of three day old beard. He began laughing absurdly, a barking noise, relieved to realize that the body before him was not Evie.

It was a man.

Again, he touched the face that he couldn't see. The nose was sharp and narrow, the hair thin and receding. A new and awful thought struck him. It had to be Edward. Eddie felt for the jugular again, tenderly, but it was as lifeless and still as the darkness around him. He tried to will the vein to throb with life but it would not. It would not respond to his deepest plea.

Eddie felt something hot and searing slip down his cheek. He knew it was a tear without touching it. He would never be able to say he was sorry to this person, sorry that he had caused him so much trouble, to tell him that he was ashamed and grieving that he had brought him to this wretched end. He dropped his hands to the figure's shoulders and shook it violently, "Edward, Edward, wake up. I'm sorry," Eddie sobbed. He turned away and heaved into the grass until his chest was on fire again, his lungs straining against cracked ribs.

"Eddie," a faint voice called his name. He pushed away from the figure. "Eddie," his name came again out of the darkness. It wasn't from the lifeless form but from a figure approaching up the hill, the way that Vickie and Nigel had gone. Was she not satisfied with the enormous prize she now had in her possession; why did she feel it necessary to come back? He was no threat to her and neither was poor Edward.

"Eddie," the voice called again. "Are you ok?"

He struggled to his feet, "Evie! Is that you?"

She was breathing heavily as she ran the last few feet. "They let me out of the car at the main road. She said she had what she wanted and I'd just slow them down. Are you ok? I can't see you very well."

"Yeah, I'm ok, but he's not." Eddie motioned unseen toward Edward.

"The other man?"

"Edward," said Eddie. "He's dead."

"He was yelling for them to stop when they ran you down. That woman hit him very hard and then Nigel stopped the car and pushed him out. I was afraid she had killed you, too."

"Come on," Eddie said as he took her hand. "I think my ribs are broken. I can't pick him up. We'll get help and come back for him."

Chapter Twenty-One

Fairfax Manor

Sir Reginald tilted back the last few drops of his whiskey and appeared deep in his own thoughts as he set the glass back on the table. He looked at Rhetts, now fully recovered from his heart attack, and wearing his own hint of a smile. Sir Reginald looked sideways at Eddie, "Evie owes you her life and of course, Rhetts and I owe you an enormous debt of gratitude." Rhetts nodded his agreement. Sir Reginald continued, "But it would seem that your own little game has caused quite a lot of trouble and put several people at risk."

Eddie had prepared himself for this moment and realized he deserved whatever was coming. It dawned on him that he was the last of the instigators left to answer for everything. Vickie and Nigel had fled and would have to deal with each other. Poor Edward was dead and Eddie could never repay the infinite debt he owed him. Eddie accepted that he deserved whatever punishment Sir Reginald thought appropriate and wouldn't resist.

He desperately hoped it wouldn't mean losing his freedom again, but if that was to be. . . he closed his eyes as the thought sank in. He deserved it and that would be his penance and his punishment. Then he could finally think about his life as a clean slate.

Edward now had a clean slate. Sir Reginald had reluctantly agreed to allow his burial in the manor's private cemetery.

And however the two old men would manage to explain away all the events of the past few days to the authorities, Eddie could only guess. Sir Reginald was extraordinarily wealthy, had been powerful in his time and undoubtedly counted other powerful people as friends. A lot could be done with resources like that, Eddie expected, but he was in no position to ask questions.

After Sir Reginald's pronouncement of his guilt, he waited for the sentence. And then a strange thought took hold of him. He thought about the judge and wished he could tell him he was sorry, that he wished he could return all his money. But that wasn't possible, he'd given it all to Vickie.

And Vickie. . . he didn't understand what had happened to her but he hoped she regained her senses. He wouldn't wish his experience at Prestonburg on anyone... yeah. . . what she'd done was unthinkable, she was a murderer, but perhaps she was insane. . She had to be.

"Edward," Sir Reginald had addressed him by his proper name. Eddie looked up.

"I assume you are now willing to make amends," Sir Reginald looked at him evenly.

"Yes," said Eddie, without hesitation, "I am."

"Good," Sir Reginald said with a sparkle in his eye and a grin at his old friend, "I believe Rhetts still has some documents for your signature."

With his broken ribs persisting in radiating hot, sharp signals, Eddie rose slowly to his feet and looked at Sir Reginald and Rhetts. Hardly believing what they were suggesting, Eddie straightened painfully but resolutely to his full height.

"No," he said, as certain as he had ever been in his life, "I'm going home."